ALL IN GOD'S TIME

ALL IN GOD'S TIME:

Memoirs from My Life's Journey

To every purpose
there is a season...
Ecclesiastes. 3:1   As Ever,

Alphonso Washington

Rev. Alphonso Washington

As told to my wife, Carol P. Washington

Copyright © 2009 by Rev. Alphonso Washington.

ISBN: Hardcover   978-1-4415-3206-0
              Softcover   978-1-4415-3205-3

All rights reserved. No part of this book may be reproduced or transmitted in any form or by any means, electronic or mechanical, including photocopying, recording, or by any information storage and retrieval system, without permission in writing from the copyright owner.

This book was printed in the United States of America.

To order additional copies of this book, contact:
Xlibris Corporation
1-888-795-4274
www.Xlibris.com
Orders@Xlibris.com
61946

CONTENTS

Dedication and Acknowledgements 7
Forward 9
Words from the Commander 13
Prologue 15

Chapter 1—The Journey Begins—in 1913 (The First Step) 17
Chapter 2—"Grandfather and the Sunday School Proposal" 28
Chapter 3—"A Sudden Change in Character" 33
Chapter 4—"The Twenties were Rough Times for us." 37
Chapter 5—"The Ku Klux Clan make themselves known." 51
Chapter 6—"I was making big money now;
Tom Kines paid me $11.00 a month." 54
Chapter 7—"Elizabeth Ambler and Sandlot Baseball on Sunday
caused me concern!" 56
Chapter 8—"I found out the identity of several local Klan members." 63
Chapter 9—"Saved, Baptized, Preaching,
Plumbing and Dancing, uh oh!" 65
Chapter 10—"You have been chosen" 74
Chapter 11—"Church business was very different then!" 82
Chapter 12—"Education is Important" 89
Chapter 13—"The Whites Began to Help Me" 92
Chapter 14—"The Sixties Were Even Better Years" 97
Chapter 15—"Entering Politics from the 1950's through the 1990's" 113

Chapter 16—"The Eighties, more rough times but full of Change"........ 124

Chapter 17—1985-86 "The Austin Diagnostic Clinic"........................135

Chapter 18—"Changes in Both my Church and Personal life"............139

Chapter 19—2001-Present "Carry me back to old Virginia"................149

Chapter 20—"Out of Calamity comes Contentment".........................152

Chapter 21—"The Courtship is in full Swing"......................................165

Dedication and Acknowledgments

When you reach the age of 95 and are in the process of publishing your first book many of those significant people in your life have passed on to their reward. Nevertheless I would be remiss not to mention them here among the others.

In my Texas years, I want to mention my first wife, Rosa Mae, the mother of my three children and a grandson that we raised. While she was not crazy about being a pastor's wife, she was, however, the greatest asset to my pastoring and my plumbing business during the 43 years we were married before she died. She was also an asset in that she kept me abreast of all my civil work and appointments.

Next would be my children, Mabeleen, Sam and Willie. They are still a great asset to my life today. I will also mention here a grandson my first wife and I raised from 4 days old through college, Sean.

My second wife, Annie Lee gave me some of the most wonderful step-children. Even after she passed, her children were always extremely good to me.

The following men are deceased but need to be acknowledged. Mr. H. Y. Price was a man who helped me in all of my civic work and because his help reached that work, to my church work and personal life. I wish also to acknowledge Dr. Jewel, from the former Southwest Texas University of San Marcos now Texas State University-San Marcos, a great help to me while I was President of the Board of Directors for Community Action over three counties. Lastly, Dr. William Crook was very instrumental in the relocation and building of my church, First Baptist Church NBC in San Marcos.

Upon my coming home to Hume, VA, there are a number of people here I wish to acknowledge. First of all, my wife Carol; this book is really dedicated to her, my co-author, as without her, this book would not be written. Since our marriage she has assisted me in every part of my life, our marriage, our church work, our association work, and our many trips and engagements made together. She has embraced my children and their loved ones as her children have embraced me. At this time in my life she is my greatest help health wise, both emotionally and physically. Not only has she helped me in these but we have great fun together in our love of God and each other.

There are two preachers I wish to mention here as well, my pastor Dr. Lindsay O. Green, who is a biblical encyclopedia. A deep and abiding relationship exists to this day between Rev. Gillison Wanser and me. This friendship began between our wives and then extended to us.

There are a host of others who could be mentioned here if room permitted. The greatest of these would be my Poles families who have embraced me as their brother/uncle after many years of estrangement.

Alphonso Washington

Left to right: Rev. Frederick Poles, myself and brother Deacon James Poles.

FORWARD

ALPHONSO WASHINGTON CAME on the horizon of my life in 2001 at the Washington Family Reunion in the month of July. The thought crossed my mind to transport him from San Marcos, TX, for the purpose of conducting our annual fall Revival leading up to the 4th Sunday in September, the time of our annual Homecoming celebration at the Mount Morris Baptist Church in Hume, VA. As I approached Alphonso to communicate this request I was taken aback by the energetic exuberance of the 'old' man. This cemented my decision to pursue engaging him to preach our Revival.

After our initial cordial greetings I came right to the point of asking him to make the trip from San Marcos to Hume. After a moment of considering the proposition he accepted. As a result of his acceptance a chain of events followed that has revolutionized the spiritual setting of the Mount Morris Baptist Church and the community of Hume. You see, Rev. Washington left Hume with an inner turmoil from which he would not be released until his return to the community where he was born and raised.

The story of his Life's Journey will help the readers to face their private issues of past dilemmas and bring them to resolution in their own lives by applying the Grace of God. We at Mount Morris Baptist Church are thankful to God the Father of our Lord Jesus Christ for the returning of our beloved brother to the church founded and pastored by his great grandfather, Elder Cornelius Gaddis, and pastored by the grandfather who raised him during the days of his early childhood, Elder Phillip Washington.

I am personally humbled to have the distinction of being his pastor from July 7th 2002 unto this present day.

Psalm 92 KJV

*12 The righteous shall flourish like the palm tree:
he shall grow like a cedar in Lebanon.
13 Those that be planted in the house of the LORD
shall flourish in the courts of our God.
14 They shall still bring forth fruit in old age;
they shall be fat and flourishing;
15 To shew that the LORD is upright: he is my rock,
and there is no unrighteousness in him.*

Lindsay O. Green

WORDS FROM THE COMMANDER

MY DEAR FRIEND, the Reverend Alphonso Washington, has done so many good things over the many years I have known him: my own granddaughter Cathryn, now 12, was blessed and prayed over by him within hours of her birth while still in the hospital; a great number of American Legion members attended a church outside their own personal faith tradition in Rev. Washington's "fifth Sunday" program when members of the Legion Family attended various church services as a group during his many years as American Legion Post Chaplain in San Marcos, Texas; he encouraged others to be involved in ways not only in matters of faith, but also through his example of life and living. As a World War II veteran, a military-trained chaplain, Rev. Washington practiced diversity many years before it was the "politically correct" thing to do; he has been involved in his own insular community without separating himself from the wider community. He is an example of a good life, lived well.

Although I have known Rev. Washington over the years largely through our various and mutual connections as military veterans, that has been just the beginning. I also have known his work in the community, in the town, as a plumber—as a worker with his hands and his mind, and largely as an example. Over the past six years I have visited him and his new bride, Carol, (after each lost their previous spouses to death) in their home in Virginia. My wife and I have had the pleasure of taking trips with them, looking at old places which meant something during earlier periods of his life, and spending many enjoyable hours of conversation, from which I gleaned a little of his wisdom gained over his 95+ years of life. On all these occasions, he has been an inspiration.

For most of us, there are few life examples of individuals to emulate. Rev. Washington is one such example for me. There is a metaphor of the way he lives his life which is bound up in his own body. A number of years ago, his eyesight was failing and it was difficult for him to preside over services when a friend had died—due to the small print of the Holy Scriptures he was reading. I saw this and KNEW that all this was in his mind and heart, so I suggested that he skip the actual reading of scripture and simply share from his own store of wisdom. It turned out that Rev.

Washington could spout scripture more eloquently than if he were reading it, probably because he has lived it.

Years later, it turned out that Rev. Washington re-grew a lobe of a lung which had been removed for cancer. It seems that our Father was not through with him yet. This comes with much love and gratitude for the great gift of my friend, Rev. Alphonso Washington.

Thomas L. "Tom" Tvrdik, October 2008

PROLOGUE

WOODROW WILSON WAS president when I was born. He was reelected in 1916 as a peace candidate, which was the same year my mother brought me to Hume, Virginia to live with my grandfather, Elder Phillip Washington. Elder Washington was the third pastor of the Mount Morris Baptist Church. President Wilson tried to mediate between the warring nations; but when the Germans resumed unrestricted submarine warfare in 1917, Wilson brought the United States into what is now believed to have been a war that made the world safe for democracy. This may seem like just a bit of history, but it actually parallels my life in an odd way. You see, I was born on October 18, 1913 in Washington, DC, and my grandfather didn't like me at all (he was at war) but when my mother brought me to him in 1916, my innocence brought peace to our family. You see, I reminded him too much of my father and he refused to allow my parents to marry.

My life reaches back to a time when we studied by coal oil lamps and plowed fields with mules. My mother's parents became the watchful eyes guiding my early years. My grandfather, Elder Phillip Washington, was an ex-slave in Virginia, and it was from him that I first learned honesty, integrity, courage and a commitment to God and family. Always working with a system I had a zeal for hard work. My mother, Kate, greatly influenced my character as well; she was a deeply religious woman who was kind, generous and loving as well as, my father, French Poles, who was a successful farmer, cattle buyer and landowner. My father demonstrated resourcefulness and determination to grasp the American dream, which is mirrored in my life as well. I recall quite well when black men were lynched for being romantically involved with a white woman, when I struggled as a young man just to support my family, when both my mother and stepfather were invalids, when I witnessed firsthand the wrath of the Ku Klux Klan and the battle against integration. Beside the struggles, I have had many happy times too, like dancing to performances by Chick Webb's band and Ella Fitzgerald in Washington, DC. All through this life of mine, God was in control. Nevertheless, as I approached what some call 'old age' I have become comfortable in the modern world; with computers, email, cell phones and the Internet. I was probably in my late 80's when I learned to use a computer for the first time; now in my mid-nineties, I communicate regularly with my family and friends via my own email account.

I served my country, was drafted into what was then called the Army Air Force in 1942, and was immediately sent to Air Navigation School in San Marcos, TX. I remained in San Marcos for nearly sixty years. Here, I married and raised a family while fighting against the prejudice that hindered me on every hand. God was still in control. His Hand kept me through every struggle in my life, as one step led to another. This is my life; I have lived through two world wars, danced for change on the streets of Washington, DC, was threatened with a 'billy' club by a policeman, while people took my personal things, eventually built a successful business from scratch, lost two wives to cancer and am a cancer and heart attack survivor myself. Nevertheless, I believe that God allowed all that has happened to me in my life because of His greater purpose.

It is my prayer that my story will inspire readers of all ages to recognize that God has a plan and purpose for each one, different but leading to a place where He will get all the glory. He placed a call on my life from which I ran for nine years. Once I accepted the call to preach, I held onto my faith and accepted His plan, *'All in God's Time.'*

CHAPTER 1

The Journey Begins—in 1913 (The First Step)

*

FAUQUIER COUNTY HAS changed a lot in the years since I left the dirt roads. Taking a whole day to get to Warrenton, the county seat and back . . . just 20 miles away; those days are gone forever. Even though I had always missed the beautiful rolling hills of Virginia, I never thought for one minute that I would end up coming back here, to my home . . . kinda going full circle, as they say. It wasn't easy to leave the country nor was it easy to come back. You see, I was pretty tied up in Texas. Tied in many ways . . . I know you are thinking, "What does Texas have to do with Virginia?" You know the old saying is, "A journey of a thousand miles begins with a single step." Virginia to Texas and back again is a journey of over three thousand miles. You have to start by taking that first step. To explain all that, I'll have to go back to the beginning and I warn you it's been quite a journey. Don't know if you are a God-fearing man like me, but I see the Hand of God in every mile. Now I didn't always see it that way, you catch what I mean? I ran from the call of God on my life for nine years. You'll hear that again. It is said that everyone has a story to tell. This is mine.

My mother, Kate Katherine Washington was born to my grandparents, Elder Phillip and Molly Gaddis Washington. By the time I came along, on October 18, 1913 in Washington, D.C., mother already had one son, Luther Washington. My brother Luther was about 5 years older than I. Mother was 25 years old when I was born; she was born in 1888. We were in Washington because work in the country—Hume, VA was scarce and mother had three of us to support now; and Washington, DC was thriving. My father was French Poles, a stock dealer and a large landowner when he died. The fact that they never married was a big problem to me then.

Mother also was keeping Polly, whose actual name was Elizabeth. She was a great grandchild of my grandparents. We were about the same age and growing up together. When I was three years old, my mother took us, Polly and me, to Hume, Virginia, to live with my grandparents; Luther was already there in Hume. I will have much more to say about my mother and father later. Little Polly died within a month after we arrived in Hume. She was the only one I had to play with at the time and her death really bothered me, leaving me all alone. Of course, I didn't understand death.

* * *

Map of Hume, VA 22639

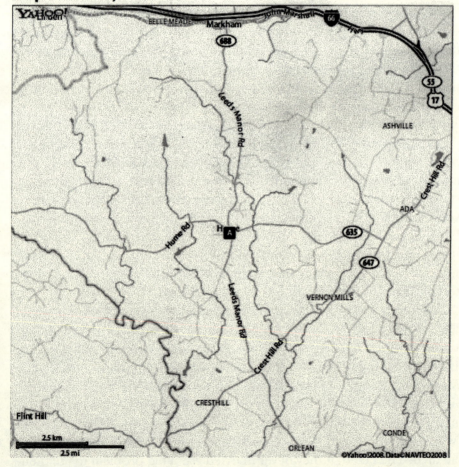

Now Hume was a farming village of mixed races, you understand. There were quite a few colored families living there and working for the white people in the area; most of the colored were sharecroppers, and some whites were too.

Describing this little village the best way I can—from memory, makes it seem like most small towns. You see, it was basically a crossroads. Leeds Manor Road (Route 688) ran North/South from Warrenton VA through Orlean to Hume and on to Markham. This road was intersected by Hume Road (Route 635), which ran East/West from Marshall to Huntly, VA. The village of Hume was located at this crossroads. The high school for the white children was located at this crossroads, sitting on the northwest quadrant of the intersection. Now there were a lot of churches here in this small area. One way or another you were going to hear the Word of God! The Hume Baptist Church (white) was just north of the school on Leeds Manor Road, and the white Episcopal Church was on the same road further north towards Markham and bore the name Leeds Episcopal. On this same road there was a golf course between the Hume Baptist and the Leeds Church. There was a farm next to the golf course owned by George Cable. The colored school, built in 1906, was located about a mile from Hume west of the village, on Hume Road. Mount Morris Primitive Baptist Church (colored) was south of Hume on Leeds Manor Road and this church was founded and built in 1867 by former slaves. There was a Presbyterian Church there east on Hume Road, just at the edge of the village. Located in the center of the business section of the village were three stores, all on Leeds Manor Road and approximately 50 houses within a radius of a mile going north, south, east, or west. Located just off the crossroads were the businesses patronized by people who lived within ten miles of the village. Folks who came from miles around attended Mount Morris Primitive Baptist Church and other churches. From the center of the village heading south was West Poe's store, a general farming building. Right at the crossroads across from the white high school was the post office located in the back of a store operated by Mr. Jim Priest, brother-in-law of Mr. Charlie Cordor, who owned it and was a prominent citizen of Hume. He owned the telephone company in Hume as well. The only doctor in the village was Dr. Rudasill, who lived on an acre of the golf course grounds near the Episcopal Church. We lived a little more than a half a mile from Hume, going east toward Marshall, VA. Hume has changed to a great extent over the years since I grew up there.

* * *

 My grandfather didn't like me at all in the beginning. According to my mother, grandfather disliked me because I was the spitting image of my daddy. My father and grandfather did not get along for some reason. My mother said grandfather did not approve of her relationship with my father; later I thought it was possibly because of their age difference—she was a bit older than he. But that was as far as it went. In those days, you didn't question those things. He liked Polly and Luther but not me . . . One day my mother brought me up to his house to stay while she went back to Washington to work; I was just a toddler at the time. He was sitting in his dining room with his Bible and my mother was in the kitchen. My grandfather could not read nor write; he knew the alphabet, and he could spell some words by sounds, but he always tried to read the bible. He was a slave and never went to school; was married and had children before the emancipation. While he was sitting there, I crawled from the kitchen to the dining room where he was sitting and laid my head on his feet (socks) and went to sleep. Mother said he looked down and saw me, instantly with a change of heart toward me. Mother said the Lord caused that to happen. He said, "Look here; I'm the only person in the house who dislikes the kid, and he comes and lays his head on my feet." From that time on a close bond developed between us, especially following my grandmother's death. He really took a great interest in me then. He took time to teach me obedience and talked to me about things I couldn't understand at the time, but things that came back to my remembrance in later years.

* * *

 My grandfather was a man who stood about six feet, nine inches tall. He could stand straight up and nearly touch his knees with his fingertips because his arms were unusually long. His hands were unusually large, and his fingers were long enough to easily hold a basketball in one hand. He was a powerful man. My paternal great-grandfather, Ned Washington, came back to Virginia following the emancipation after being sold and carried to Kentucky as a slave. Great-Grandfather Ned lived in a cabin up on a hill on the same property my grandfather farmed. This was on the old Stribling place that he had worked for and bought. In fact, my grandfather showed me a chimney that belonged to the house where my great grandfather Ned had lived. The house had long since disappeared, but the chimney was still standing when I was a boy.

My grandfather was adding a room onto his house and had two white carpenters helping him. It began to rain while he had a pile of lumber out in the yard. He started to carry the lumber in the house and the two carpenters were not helping but were in deep conversation or arguing about some trifling matter; consequently, they didn't notice him moving the lumber inside. Suddenly he surprised them when he stepped between them and lifted both of them off the ground, butted their heads, and dropped them, without saying a word. Together these men weighed at least 350 pounds. He went back to his task of moving the lumber. The two startled carpenters quit arguing and rushed to help with the lumber. Another incident showing my grandfather's unusual strength came after we had loaded a wagon with sacks of wheat we had threshed and were carrying to the mill in Delaplane, VA. In the course of riding there in a horse drawn wagon, the back wheels became uncoupled from the front. My grandfather got down under the wagon and with his legs and feet up against the bottom of the wagon, he raised it up enough to re-couple the wagon wheels. A fully loaded wagon like this was unbelievably heavy. But grandfather was a powerfully strong man.

He worked hard on his farm, expecting his mules and horses to work hard, too. The people in the Hume community all worked together when harvest time came. Once one farm was harvested, they all went to the next. During wheat cutting season, we would have four horses pulling a wheat binder. My grandfather's youngest son, Uncle George helped him work the harvest. There was one horse on each side of the binder's "tongue," with two horses up in front of them. The two in front were hooked to a chain on the end of the tongue. The horse on the left side of the tongue was called the saddle horse; Uncle George was riding this horse. The horse on the right side of the tongue was called the "off-side" horse. Sometimes the "off-side" horse wouldn't be pulling like it was supposed to pull. Grandfather didn't like that at all, saying to his son, "George, make that horse pull!" Uncle George would tap the horse with the whip. The horse would pull for a few rounds of the wagon and then stop pulling again. Grandfather said, "I'm tired of that horse, he is just walking along and the other three are pulling the load." So, he cut off a long switch from a tree and stood back, watching the horse awhile. Grandfather walked up to the wagon, reached across Uncle George whipping the stubborn horse with the switch. But the switch was cutting Uncle George across the back at the same time it was striking the horse. After that whipping with the switch, that horse would be pulling every time; all grandfather had to do from then on was look at him. I never will forget that day! Uncle George was trying to dodge the switch, but my grandfather was determined to teach that horse a lesson, and Uncle George just happened to be in the way. Grandfather was the type of man who didn't tell you to do something but once.

* * *

We attended the Mount Morris Primitive Baptist Church on Leeds Manor Road. My maternal grandfather, Rev. Cornelius Gaddis, was the founder and first pastor of this church. During the time I was under my grandfather's care, he pastored Mount Morris Baptist Church for a year... 1916-1917. This church had a profound effect on my life both in the beginning and toward the end.

My Grandmother Molly, great grandfather Gaddis' oldest daughter, was a short dark-skinned woman who was loved dearly by all her grandchildren. One thing I remember in particular about her was that whenever one of us was stung by a bee or wasp, we would run straight to Grandmother Molly. Regardless of who else was in the house, we grandchildren wanted her to rub some medicine on the sting. We felt that if grandmother didn't do it, it wouldn't work. Her love and attention to us made us feel this way. She was a kind, loving woman with a positive attitude. She was also an expert quilt maker. She invited her friends to join her in making quilts from scraps of cloth. Prayer was always a big part of her life and before the quilting work would get started, one of the women would offer up a prayer. When my grandmother prayed, I could tell she was coming to the end of her prayer when she would always reference a time when she would "drink down her last cup of sorrow and wind up her last ball of trouble." More than eighty seven years later, I still use those same words in my own prayers from time to time. She died when I was eight years old, but I can remember people preparing her body for burial. The custom in those days was to have the body laid out at home. On the day of the funeral, the coffin was carried to the cemetery in a "Spring Wagon," which was a wagon with a seat up front on a flat bed with sides approximately eight inches high.

* * *

When my grandfather worked for Mr. Jim Stribling, it was in exchange for approximately twenty-five acres of farmland. They had a verbal agreement, because Mr. Stribling promised him verbally that if he worked for him for a number of years, the twenty-five acres would be deeded to him. However, at the end of the designated years, Mr. Stribling refused to honor his agreement. Because my grandfather could not read nor write, he didn't know that Mr. Stribling had been giving him worthless pieces of paper for receipts. When my grandfather thought his time was up he took the papers to Mr. Stribling to collect on the agreement. Mr. Stribling told him there was nothing about their agreement on these papers. Now there was nothing Grandfather could do to force him to give him the deed to the property. Mr. Stribling had the upper hand on my grandfather; he assured him that if he would work for him a little longer, he would get the twenty-five acres. Grandfather agreed to this new proposal, feeling there was no other option. However this time, he let one of his children who could read, keep up with the receipts to avoid being cheated for the second time. Grandfather eventually got the deed to his farm. Uncle George lived on eleven acres of an adjoining farm up the hill from my grandfather's place, which was owned by Claudie Lea. This place was in some kind of debt with back taxes owed and she told my grandfather that if he would straighten it out then he could have the deed. My grandfather did this and I went with him on the trip to Warrenton to straighten this out; the property was deeded to my grandfather.

Grandfather raised wheat, barley, vegetables, tobacco, and other crops, but he didn't have enough land to plant all the corn he wanted to grow, so he rented some acreage on the Stribling farm. He would get three fifths of the corn, and Mr. Stribling would get two-fifths, according to their share cropping arrangement. They would cut down the corn and put it in shocks. An acre could produce twelve shocks of corn. So, my grandfather would get three shocks and Mr. Stribling would get the next two. Grandfather would haul Mr. Stribling's share of the corn first and put it in his corn crib. Then he would load his own share on the wagon and take it to his barn on the farm. There was always an abundance of livestock on the farm, including horses, cows, hogs, chickens, and turkeys; actually the farm produced all of the food that our large family needed.

Because grandfather didn't have enough space to plant his beans in a separate field, he planted navy beans with the corn. The hills of corn were three feet apart; in every other hill he would plant beans and the beans would run up the corn. With a tool called a replanter, he would drop beans in each hole. Once you planted your crop with a planter, you couldn't go back with that equipment to replant places where the seed didn't come up. I haven't seen a replanter in over 87 years.

Let me tell you about this corn planter, it had two wheels on it with a box on each side. There was a chain with notches on it that stretched across the field. The chain had to be moved to keep up with the planting. This would take usually two people to do the planting. The planter had a marker with a pivot that made the marks that kept the rows straight. The chain had to be pulled tight consistently to keep the rows straight. Believe me, this took some skill to accomplish. Pulling the chain was my job. I would grab the pole and pull it over to the other side, get that chain and pull it two or three times and stick the iron peg in the ground. When I first started helping grandfather with the planting, I didn't stick the iron peg deep enough in the ground, and the horse would pull it up. He would holler "boy!" He didn't whip me, but he scolded me pretty bad. Then I had to go back and stick it back down again. Now that was work! Nobody can tell you different; that was really hard work! At the same time though, I had a feeling that I was helping; a sense of pride. "Boy, I worked today!" I would think to myself. It made me feel like I was worth something. Boys who didn't have to do farm work, boys who just ran the streets, were not respected like those of us who worked on the farm.

* * *

My grandparents, Phillip—born in 1851 and Molly—born in 1857, had 13 children of their own, and they both raised their younger siblings in the household with their children. Grandfather had four siblings, Joe, Charlie, Mariah and Lettie; Grandmother Molly had two or three siblings. They took on this responsibility soon after the emancipation. They had been "put together" as husband and wife while very young during slavery, when they were separated from their parents. My mother was the fourth youngest of their children. Aunt Martha and Uncle George were the two children between my mother and Aunt Carrie. Aunt Louiza was the oldest child that they had. She died in a house fire long before I was born. I learned that she got her children out safely, but went back in the house to get something. She got out of the house alive, but died a short while after the fire. Aunt Louiza's baby child was named Raymond. He was my first cousin, but he was older than Aunt Carrie. She was my guardian at this time. When she got married and left with her husband, moving to Philadelphia PA, my grandfather took care of me.

Grandfather worked for the Southern Railroad, building the railroad by driving steel spikes into the ties to hold the rails to the tracks. He did most of his traveling by train because he had a pass that allowed him to ride free. He used to pin a note on me when I was five to ten years old and homesick for my mother. He would put me on the train at Markham VA to travel to Washington, DC to visit my mother and my older brother Luther. I used his rail pass. Back then there was the 7th Street Train Station; mother would meet me there when I got off the train, which went on to Union Station. There was a streetcar track on 7th right there where I got off the train. Mother lived on Florida Avenue. We would get on the streetcar and it would drop us off right in front of my mother's house. To send me back to Hume, my mother would repeat this action in reverse. My mother had to work so I couldn't stay long in Washington. I didn't like Washington anyway, there was no place to play ball where my mother lived. I have always said to this day, Washington DC is a good place to be 'from'.

* * *

When we needed flour my Grandfather would take a load of wheat to the mill in Delaplane where he would exchange it for a big barrel of flour. I went with grandfather once and it was an all day trip. From before day till after dark, we made this trip and I really felt like a man, like I was really doing something when I was with him. I really did nothing but get hungry and he would stop at a little store on the way and buy us some sardines in flat cans with a key and crackers. When we got home we would unload the flour and unhook the horses, putting them up in the barn. Grandfather kept the flour in the hallway of the new part of the house. I mention the new part of the house because that house used to be a log cabin with two rooms—one upstairs and one down. He built four rooms onto that house. We had six rooms now and while he built a bathroom in it, we never did get any plumbing installed. In the winter, he would slaughter twelve to fifteen hogs. After the hogs were butchered and cleaned, the meat would be salted down and wrapped in cloth sacks from the cement store in Marshall. See, in them days cement didn't come in paper sacks, they came in cloth sacks and grandfather would buy the empty sacks for the meat. The meat would then be hung up in the meat house to cure for several months. The cured meat was kept in the meat house in the back yard. We ground up the meat by hand and then my grandmother would fry pan sausage and put it in Mason jars. She poured the meat grease over the sausage, then she turned the jars upside down to let the grease cool, creating an airtight seal. The jars would be stored in the cool cellar. Grandfather loved to have cake or wine in the house when company came. We really had it all the time because he made dandelion wine, potato wine, and several varieties of grape wine, which he kept on the top shelf in the cellar. I don't remember a time when there was not a cake or wine in that house. The wines were kept in stone crock jugs; most of them were gallon jugs, and on the bottom shelves he kept preserves, jellies, and their canned fruits and vegetables.

* * *

As soon as we were old enough to dress ourselves, grandfather would make a call from downstairs:

"Time to get up!
The cat for the second time washes her face;
To lie in bed longer would be a disgrace.
The coffee's all ready to pour in the cup;
All who wants breakfast will have to get up."

Each of us had a morning chore that we had to do before breakfast. Grandfather would go to the barn to feed and water the livestock. By the time he came back to the house, the breakfast would be on the table. Grandmother or one of us would have to milk the cows. We would bring the milk back for breakfast. That milk was too hot to drink so it would go in the well and cold milk would come out for our breakfast drink. We didn't have an icehouse. When we all sat at the table Grandfather said a prayer. There was no waiting on you; you had to be there. At the table after grandfather finished his prayer, he picked up his plate and filled it with food and passed it to the next one to him doing this with everyone's plate until his came up last. There was no asking what you wanted; unless everything on your plate was gone did you have a chance to ask for more of anything.

When apples came in, we would get the apples and bring them to the house and peel them. After we sliced them and put a white sheet on top of the tin roof of one of the buildings like the chicken house, we spread the slices out on the roof letting the sun dry them. We did that over two or three days but if it rained we would have to get them up and do this all over again. We had to get them up before the rain or they would sour if they got wet. They had to be dry. Once they were dry we put them up, sometimes in jars and sometimes in crock jars . . . we had dried apples and that was real good eating in winter when grandmother would cook them. I loved to eat them for breakfast with pan sausage, the way my Grandmother or whoever was fixing breakfast made them. They would take the unpeeled apples (not dry ones) and put them in bacon grease in a frying pan on the stove. We ate slab bacon from our hogs. When the apples were almost fried, the juice from the apples would make syrup. Then they would sprinkle brown sugar or syrup on the apples after they had finished frying and then put them in the oven. The sugar would make a crust. Whoopee! That was good eating! The children had to give thanks for our food.

Everybody in the house had a chore to perform after breakfast. My job was to take out the chamber pots every morning. You could forget to do your chore if you wanted to, but you wouldn't forget it again! Grandfather would see to that. We had so many chores to do at the house and they had to get done.

At my house in Hume, when my brother James Burrell came to visit we used to sleep in the same room. One night during the summer, I got up to go to the outhouse, but I didn't put on any clothes. You know people don't go outdoors in their underclothes in the city. James was used to living in Washington, D.C. When he saw me go out with no clothes on he jumped up and ran into Grandfather's room and said, "Granddaddy, Granddaddy! Alphonso is outdoors in his naked meat self!" Boy that tickled me!

CHAPTER 2

"Grandfather and the Sunday School Proposal"

*

MY GRANDFATHER HAD a very close friend from Nashville TN who came to visit over a period of years. This man was Henry Boyd and he was the founder of the Boyd Publishing Company in Nashville, a religious publisher. He came to visit him quite a few times to promote Sunday school literature for the churches in the Association. Grandfather and he came to be good friends from their days in slavery for the rest of their lives. He really understood my grandfather's desire that while he was uneducated because of his past slavery, he wanted his congregation to be educated. He took great pains to introduce to my grandfather the value of the Sunday school program. Grandfather allowed me to be present at these meetings, which made a profound impression on me that remains with me until now. Henry Boyd began coming to our house before grandmother died.

My Grandfather was the pastor of Mount Morris Primitive Baptist Church from 1916-17, when Henry started to visit. Later the pastor was James Bailey. During this time my grandfather served as an Area Minister in the 2nd National Ketoctan Primitive Baptist Association of which Mount Morris was the Mother church. He would visit various churches and make reports at the Union Meetings twice a year. The Primitive Baptist Association conducted its business at its Union Meetings. Grandfather always attended the winter meeting. Other meetings were held outside of Hume. He couldn't read, but he had to deal with a lot of people who could read. Some of them tried to embarrass him, and that really bothered me. One incident that I remember involves an idea that he brought before the association. I don't remember the year that this incident occurred, but it was after he finished serving as the pastor, I think it was around 1923 because it was after my grandmother died in 1922 and Aunt Carrie had

Mount Morris Primitive Baptist Church, Hume VA. Photo compliments of the 100-year anniversary book—1867-1967

married and moved away. I was with Grandfather everywhere he went. He took me with him to the Association and Union meetings. I know Grandfather told the delegates that he believed the Primitive Baptists should organize a Sunday school. Eight of the delegates got up and walked out of the meeting to express their rejection of my grandfather's proposal because of his lack of education. What he lacked, he wanted for others. Because he didn't have the opportunity, he wanted the members to have it. Truly because my Grandfather had a lot of influence in the community among black and white people, those delegates didn't want to get into an argument with him about the Sunday school proposal, so they just walked out on him. However, soon after Grandfather died, Spotsal Brown, of the Association, introduced the same proposal that my grandfather had made and got the support and approval of all eight of the delegates who had rejected Grandfather's idea. Seeing how they treated my grandfather caused me to have a great deal of negative feelings toward preachers, the primitive Baptist church and the Association. The only two preachers I had any respect for were Grandfather and my Uncle Willie Washington.

Uncle Willie and Willie Gibbs preached their first sermons on the same day at Mount Morris Baptist Church and I was there.

* * *

I believe Grandfather was pastor of Mt. Morris for only one year because he couldn't read or write. The minister who came after him, Rev. James Bailey, was a very smart educated man who *could* read and write. In those days pastors usually stayed at a church until they died; that's why it is odd that Grandfather only served one year as pastor. Rev. Bailey was a short man who had one shoulder that was higher than the other; he was a light-brown skinned man with straight hair. He lived in Washington, D.C. and drove seventy-two miles to Hume on the fourth Sunday every month for services. Sometimes, he would come in on a Friday and stay at a church member's house. He would do this because we had church meetings on Saturday before fourth Sunday each quarter.

Even though Grandfather was pastor for only one year, he remained a faithful member, serving the church wherever he was needed. He raised a vegetable garden specifically for Mt. Morris Church to help feed delegates during the Union meetings. If Grandmother Molly took any vegetables from the garden that he planted for the church, she had to inform him so that he could replace the items with produce from his family garden. He did not want to cut the church short by taking vegetables from the church garden for his family. When he made a commitment to the church, he took it seriously. That's just the kind of man my grandfather was. Eight lost souls came to know the Lord during his short pastorate.

My grandfather was a fearless man who was well respected in Hume. To demonstrate more of his character I want to tell you this little story about him that highlights it. A riot started in the village of Hume, involving the mailman, my Uncle George, about a dozen black people and a couple of dozen white people. Our mailman was William Roberts, a black crippled man who walked with a crutch. Now William carried a concealed gun. One day, he forgot to call Meredith Royston, a white man, "Mr." Now William was a whole lot older than Royston. Then Meredith and Charlie Cordor got together to teach the mail carrier a lesson. Arthur Summers, Dee Summers, and my Uncle George Washington ended up getting involved. They were not going to let the white men whip William

FORMER PASTORS

Elder Mark Russell
Pastor 1895-1915

Elder Phillip Washington
Pastor 1916-1917

Elder William Gibbs
Pastor 1937-1945

* * *

as they had planned to do. The confrontation started to get out of hand. My uncle saw the crowd getting bigger and he went home and to get his pistol. When he came to the house and got his .38, Aunt Louise, his wife, got upset and hollered down the hill and told my Grandfather what was going on. Grandfather went from his house up to the Hume crossroads. With me close by behind him, he went up to Uncle George immediately when we reached the crowd. He just walked into the crowd and straight to my uncle and said "George, give me the gun." Uncle George knew better than to disobey his father. Grandfather walked over to Dee and said, "Hand me that knife." He then walked around and collected all the weapons, and he gave the crowd a direct order, "Now, y'all go home! I have the weapons now, and I will use them if I need to! So, y'all go home!" He was speaking to the white folks as well as the black. He said to the white people standing there, "You want to run over these young boys and I won't stand for it." Nobody argued with him. The crowd dispersed without any challenge to his moral authority. He calmed that riot down because he was not scared to step into that situation and take charge *and* because the people, black and white, respected him.

* * *

Aunt Louise and Uncle George didn't attend church regularly, but every morning without fail, he would go to a hill above his house and pray. I could hear him praying aloud, calling upon the Lord. I never knew him to join a church. However, when he attended church, Uncle George would lead the singing and offer a prayer. He had a beautiful voice and so did Aunt Louise. Other than my mother and Aunt Martha, the men were the ones who would start the songs. Uncle George would kill a calf or hog and donate and cook the meat for the church during union meetings. When he died in 1943, I had just gotten my first furlough in the Air Force and was coming to Hume for a visit. Uncle George died about an hour before I arrived in Hume. The undertaker picked up his body shortly before I got to the house. His funeral was held at Mount Morris Primitive Baptist Church where his father and grandfather had both served as pastors.

I remember another incident in which Grandfather demonstrated that he was not afraid of the white folks. Meredith Royston's father, John lived down the hill from us. He raised light brown colored turkeys and we had the old dark brown turkeys. Grandfather raised hundreds of turkeys (he would slaughter them, pick them and pack them in wooden barrels to ship to Bradshaw, the owner of a meat company in Pennsylvania. Mr. Royston's turkeys got mixed up with our turkeys one evening, and all the turkeys went up to roost after sundown. Mr. Ralston's sons Clarence and Raymond came to get their turkeys, but Grandfather said, "Boys, you should have come to get those turkeys earlier. It's too late now. They are all up in the trees roosting. You have to come back tomorrow." Clarence told Grandfather, "Daddy sent us after these turkeys, and I'm going to get them tonight!" Grandfather said, "Boy, I told you to let them turkeys alone!" He pulled off his belt and grabbed Clarence and whipped him on the spot. Raymond, the other boy who had come to help Clarence get the turkeys, ran home. Grandfather turned Clarence loose and walked on down to Mr. Royston's house and knocked on the door. He said, "I came here to tell you I whipped Clarence and I was going to whip Raymond if I could get my hands on him." Mr. Royston said, "What happened, Phil?" Granddad said "I told Clarence to leave them turkeys alone till tomorrow." Mr. Royston looked at Clarence and Raymond and said "Now, you boys know better than to not mind Uncle Phil." "Phil, they won't bother you anymore." Grandfather turned around and came on back to the house.

CHAPTER 3

"A Sudden Change in Character"

*

MY AUNT CARRIE was such a great help to me, teaching me everything at home because I stuttered; she helped me with that problem at the same time. Usually children started with the primer grade. I skipped both primer and the first grade, and later on I skipped 5th grade. My aunt had helped me overcome my stuttering problem, and she also helped other children at school who had speech impediments.

We started school in September if we were not working on a harvest, because we lived in a farming community. The children helped their parents get the crops out of the fields. I attended the Hume School for Colored Children. Back then the teachers in the colored schools were paid about a tenth of what the white teachers made. My first teacher was Miss Gussie Julius. It was not long before the news was out that my mother and father were not married. I became a target child. The boys would hang around at the end of school or during recess just to call me names and beat me up.

These boys in my school would come after me, picking on me and calling me a bastard. They beat me up after school because I wouldn't fight. I believed this was against everything I learned from my grandparents. I would try to get home before they caught me. One day I ran and didn't make it home before they got a hold of me. By the time they caught me I was near my Grandfather's house and they beat me up pretty bad. As I walked around the corner of our house I saw Grandfather standing in the yard. Blood was running out of my nose and mouth and my grandfather looked at me and asked, "Boy what happened to you?" I was trying to tell him through my crying and sniffling. He just said, "Go on in the house and let your grandmother clean you up." He was referring to my step-grandmother. My grandfather had remarried after grandmother Mollie died in 1922. His second wife was Harriet Thompson, who lived on an adjacent farm. She might have been married before because she had two daughters named, Margaret and Josephine. Ms. Harriet cleaned me up and sent me back out to my grandfather. He looked me directly in the eyes and said, "Boy, if you go to the schoolhouse and let the boys beat you up, I'm gonna beat you again when you get home."

The very next day, after school was dismissed, the boys said, "You told on us, didn't you?" This statement caused me to I tear out running, and they took out behind me. I was almost home as they closed in on me. There was a bank on the other side of the road from my house. My house was on the lower side of the hill. I ran up on the bank to get away from these boys. The boys involved in the fight included James Smith, Andrew Clay and my cousin Robert Louis Washington, Uncle Neely's son, and a bunch of other boys. I looked out across the road to my house, and there stood my grandfather in the yard, looking straight at us. Then it hit me; he's going to whip me. I happened to look down on the ground where I was standing and saw wooden spokes from a broken wagon wheel. I picked up two of those spokes one in each hand, and I hit every one of the boys who came toward me. Man, I was just piling them up; everyone I hit would fall to the ground and just lie there. Grandfather didn't say anything about the fight when I came home.

Right after sundown fathers began to arrive at the house in buggies and on horseback. It looked like we were having a church meeting. I went and hid in the hall away from my grandfather because I knew why they were coming. I was listening through the keyhole to what was going on in the front room. I knew I wasn't allowed in the room where the grown folks were talking. The fathers of the boys involved in the fight were coming to talk to Grandfather about what I'd done to their boys. He was meeting them at the door, greeting them so nice and politely. Whenever visitors came to the house, he always offered them wine and a big slice of cake or pie. This was no different to him. We had cakes and pies in the house. He called his wife and told her, "Daught, get some cake and wine." He had a large grape arbor on the farm, and he made grape wines. For some unbeknownst reason to me, Grandfather called both of his wives "Daught." While eating and drinking the men told him what had happened to their sons earlier that day. I felt bad to hear that I had hit Robert above his left eye because he was my first cousin. Grandfather listened to all the reports; then he said, "Well, gentlemen, yesterday that boy [talking about me] came home, and he was so beat up he had blood running from his nose, ears, and mouth. I saw that for myself. And when

I talked to my wife about it, she said that wasn't the first time that Fonso had come home bleeding from a beating at the hands of those boys. Right then, I told my grandson if he let those boys beat him up again, I was going to whip him when he came home. And this evening, they ran him up on that bank. I witnessed this myself. He defended himself just like I told him to do. And I stand behind the boy!" I never heard anything more about the fight. The men accepted his explanation without any further discussion and left.

This whole experience taught me that I could fight with the support of my grandfather. But you could say I got out of control. Spelling bees in school really brought out the worst in me. I became aggressive, as the students lined up on opposite walls of the school room, and because I still stuttered a bit, my classmates didn't always understand me. I would spell a word correctly, but somebody would say, "That ain't right!" Then the teacher would call the same word to the other side and the student would spell it the same way I had spelled it. I would say "that's the way I spelled it!" You better not disagree with me or I would hit you hard as I could. You had to be in the teacher's lap to keep me from hitting you. My friend, Gladys Washington would say, "That boy will kill you!" When I found out I could fight, if my hand wouldn't stop you, I was going to get something to stop you! I didn't care how big you were, I was going to stop you! I think Gladys was afraid of me then.

* * *

A mildly retarded boy, Harry Clay was in class and being disruptive to our teacher, Miss Ada Watts. They got into an argument and she asked him to leave the room. Mose Clay who was older than Harry—about 18 years old, became angry with Miss Watts, throwing an inkwell at her, striking her behind the ear. She fell to the floor unconscious. Then Lucy Settles, also an older student, took charge of the situation and dismissed the school staying behind looking after the wounded teacher. Mose was eventually sent to prison for assaulting Miss Watts.

In the fourth grade, I won first place in the school spelling bee, with the winning word, "chrysanthemum." Annie Whitmore, a sixth grader, was the best speller in the school, but she somehow missed that word. She was so embarrassed about losing to a fourth grader that she went home crying and never came back to the school.

Even though I stayed in Hume until my grandfather died in 1926, the year I turned 13 years old, I want to include here what happened to me when my mother brought me back to Washington after Grandfather's funeral.

* * *

While I was attending school in Washington, DC, one of my teachers, Mrs. Mann, principal of the school, provided a scholarship for me to enroll at the Hampton Institute. However, my mother and stepfather became ill, making it impossible for me to accept the scholarship. I had to work to help support my family. Sometime later, I met Mrs. Mann on Pennsylvania Avenue. I had a misconception regarding Miss Mann. She was so hard on me in school I thought she didn't like me. Naturally when I met her on the street I was curious about why she made a way for me to have this scholarship. Feeling pretty bold, I said, "Mrs. Mann, I want to ask you a question that has been on my mind since I left school. Why did you give me a scholarship to Hampton Institute even though you didn't like me?" She looked at me square in the eye and said: "Young man, I thought the world of you. I recognized your potential, and I didn't want you to be influenced by students who were not interested in getting an education. That's why I was hard on you."

Certainly I had misinterpreted Mrs. Mann's motives for giving me extra work in school. I thought she did it to punish me or because she didn't like me. I was both pleased to hear her explanation and very embarrassed to have questioned her goodwill toward me and hoped to never meet her again, I felt so bad.

CHAPTER 4

"The Twenties were Rough Times for us."

*

I WAS BETWEEN ten and 12 years old before my mother told me who my father was. I am not sure if the beatings and name calling from my classmates had anything to do with her decision to tell me when she did. This is how it happened; the events that led up to her telling me.

My grandmother died when I was eight, and Grandfather remarried approximately two years later. Sometime during the period after my grandmother died, Grandfather and I were living together at the house in Hume. Aunt Carrie, Grandfather's youngest daughter, was living with us and helping Grandfather to take care of me. She was always good about looking after me. It was during this time that Aunt Carrie got married. Grandfather performed the wedding right there in his house. After the wedding, Aunt Carrie and her husband moved to Philadelphia, Pennsylvania as I mentioned before. Grandfather was still a widower. Soon after Aunt Carrie left, my mother came from Washington to visit us. She stayed about two weeks making sure Grandfather could manage the household and take care of me. She brought her other children with her, James and Molly, but Luther had died.

* * *

Earlier, when my grandmother died, (I was about 8 years old) Luther went back to D.C. to live with our mother, leaving Aunt Carrie and me with Grandfather. According to my mother, Luther bought some popcorn and a bottle of Orange Crush soda water on his way to the picture show. In those days, they didn't sell popcorn and soda water in the theater. You had to buy your snacks in a store next door to the theater. He drank the soda water, but he got sick in the theater and went home before the movie was over. Mother said he came home and got in the bed. Later that night, he began to feel worse. He was sick two or three hours before a doctor arrived to treat him. Mother had to go down to a phone on the corner to call the doctor. The doctor gave Luther some medicine, but he didn't put him in the hospital which was just around the corner from where they were living. Mother said the next morning Luther woke up and said he wanted to eat. Mother told him to stay in bed, and she would bring him something. She fixed him some food and he ate it.

She picked up the plate and left him sitting on the side of the bed. A little later she went back into his room and found him in the bed. She asked him, "How are you feeling?" "I'm feeling pretty good right now," he said. She said, "I'm going to call the doctor to ask if I should carry you to the hospital." She came back to his room about ten minutes later and found him dead. He was 14 years old. The doctor conducted a test that indicated that Luther died of ptomaine poisoning caused by the Orange Crush. All the neighbors heard about the cause of Luther's death, and they wanted my mother to sue the soda company. But mother refused to sue the company. She based her decision on I Corinthians 6:1, which reads, "Dare any of you, having a matter against another, go to law before the unjust, and not before the saints?" My mother knew the Bible very well. Rev. Willie Gibbs, Associate Minister at Mount Morris Baptist Church, conducted the funeral. Because the pastor of the church was out of town, Rev. Gibbs would not allow Luther's body to be taken inside the building. The service was held outside on the church grounds with burial in Grandfather's family plot. My mother was very disappointed about the way the funeral was handled, but she accepted Rev. Gibbs' decision.

The Orange Crush bottling company paid for all the funeral expenses, including the cost of shipping the body to Hume, where Luther was buried. The doctor wanted mother to sue the company, too. He informed the company of the cause of Luther's death, and that's why the company volunteered to pay for the funeral. Mother told me herself that she would not take the Orange Crush people to court.

* * *

Luther was well known in the D.C. neighborhood where he and mother lived. When I went to live with my mother years later, people still remembered Luther Eugene. My brother had worked at Frank Kidwell's grocery store as a delivery boy. Customers would call the store and order groceries on their accounts, and Luther would load the items in his red Express Wagon and make the deliveries. [The word "Express" was written on the side of the wagon.] I would later use this wagon in my work for the same grocery store!

Mother suffered a great tragedy in Washington DC when my brother Luther died, not only in his death but the manner in which his funeral was carried out. The last two years of his life he lived with her; they spent much time together but I never knew if she told him who his father was. We all knew he favored Rev. Gibbs but you just didn't talk about those things in those days, so *we* never knew. He was so close to her, like her right hand; even though he was in school he worked hard to help support my stepfather, James, Molly and her. However she decided to tell *me* who my father was when she came back to Hume.

* * *

Mother had gone back to Washington DC when my grandfather died, when I was almost thirteen years old. She took me with her; but for a long time I held myself responsible for grandfather's death. Later, I came to understand that God controls our destiny. On the morning of the event that I believed might have caused the illness that led to his death, he had planned to go to the store in Marshall, Virginia, which is about twelve miles from Hume. After he hitched his wagon and horses, he told me, "Son, I want you to go over there to the Stribling Bottom and clean up some of that brush. You can start cutting the brush while I'm gone." I walked over to the bottom, carrying a scythe and an extra long-handled three-pronged fork. Some of the brush contained thorny blackberry vines, and I used the fork to handle that kind of brush. I imagine it was around 9:30 a.m. when I got started on the brush-clearing job. Grandfather had not left on his trip to Marshall. I piled up some brush and decided to burn it. I had some matches because I had been smoking secretly since about eight, making cigarettes from tobacco that Grandfather grew on the farm. About thirty minutes after I started burning the brush, a wind came up and the fire was quickly out of control. At almost the same moment, Grandfather came over the hill on his way to Marshall; he saw the fire and yelled, "Boy, put that fire out!" I did my best to put it out, but the wind was too strong; the fire spread rapidly. Grandfather jumped out of his wagon and tried to help me put out the fire. A few minutes later, I looked around and saw 8 or 10 people from the neighborhood that had noticed the fire and had come to help fight it. We used brush to beat the fire out. The heat and smoke made fighting the fire very uncomfortable. Despite our efforts to put it out, the fire burned up to the road, but it didn't jump to the other side. It burned up all the brush and some 20 or 30 rails on a rail fence. Granddad didn't fuss at me about the fire.

The old man worked very hard trying to put out that fire. He didn't go to Marshall that day. And three or four days later he took sick. The fire occurred in the last few days of May, and Grandfather died between the 8th and 10th day of June in 1926. I blamed myself for Granddad's illness and death. I believed that if he had not had to fight that fire, he would not have died. I knew that setting that fire was the wrong thing to do, but when I started the fire, there was no wind to blow it out of control. Old Dr. Rudasill was called to treat Granddad, but he could do nothing for him. A few days later, when the adults in the house realized that Grandfather had died, Uncle George was sent to get Dr. Rudasill. The doctor examined him and pronounced him dead around 10:00 in the morning. All of Granddad's children and most of his grandchildren were in the house on the morning that he died. Mr. Kerns, the local white funeral director for blacks and whites in Hume, was called to pick up the body. Rev. Bailey, pastor of Mt. Morris Primitive Baptist Church, preached the funeral. Many people, black and white, attended my grandfather's funeral because he was so well known in Hume and highly respected. He was buried in the family plot.

The 54th Annual Session of the Second National Ketcoctan Association was held at 1st Zion Baptist Church in Edgemont PA opening on Thursday, August 19 through Sunday August 22, 1926. According to the minutes taken for the Association, there was a memorial held for my grandfather. Taken right out of the minute book the words are penned thusly:

"Saturday Afternoon Session August 21st 1926:

Council convened according to adjournment singing hymn 387 by Elder Benjamin Layton of VA. Scripture Lesson 1st John 3rd Chapter was read by Elder James Bailey of VA. Prayer by Elder Walker Carter of VA, after which the Moderator (Elder Louis Brown) stated that the service would be a memorial service for the late Elder Phillip Washington, one of our beloved Elders who had passed away, Elder James Bailey, his pastor, spoke first concerning him. Taking as his text, 1st John 2:3, which he portrayed it very beautiful in the way of applying it to the life of the deceased, and also was edifying to the saints. He was followed by Elder Benjamin Layton who stated that he had known Elder Phillip Washington for a long time and that he was a man of his word, and a soldier of the cross, and a soldier in deed. He spoke very beautiful as possible concerning his Christian life as a minister of the Gospel. The Moderator Elder Lewis Brown made some brief remarks of him concerning his truthfullness and faithfullnes in the cause of our Lord and Saviour Jesus Christ."

* * *

My mother and Grandfather's other children had come home for the funeral, but on the day of the funeral, I went back to D.C. with my mother. We lived at 1427 C Street N. E. I attended Paine Elementary School, a large urban school. It was a big red brick schoolhouse, teachers everywhere. One thing for sure, I had never seen a school that large. The only two high schools for the colored in Washington at that time were Armstrong and Dunbar. Cordoza was still in the planning stages.

When the time came, I was supposed to attend Armstrong High School, but by then both my mother and stepfather were invalids; she could walk around, but she was sick. We found out later that she had cancer in the form of tumors that kept re-occurring. Because of her illness, mother couldn't work to support us. By October, before we went back to Hume, my mother and my stepfather both had been in the hospital. I worked for Frank Kidwell's, a D.C. chain of grocery stores, trying to make ends meet, but I couldn't earn enough to feed the family. My brother James and I used to tap dance in front of the Rosalet Theater on Fourth and a Half street in Washington. Now he was better than me because he could sing too! Patrons would give us change. This little bit of money added to what we made at work would not pay our rent. Soon we had to move from NE Washington to SE. Our family was now living on the second floor of a three-story building at 725 Springman's Court during this time. A streetcar went all the way up 7th Street and I would get off at 14th Street and walk to New York Avenue to work in the Bond Building.

* * *

About the year 1928, I was the elevator operator in the old Bond Building at Fourteenth and New York Avenue; this was where J. Edgar Hoover worked. He was the one who signed our checks. I got fired from that job when I accidentally ran the elevator into the basement floor. I wasn't paying attention to what I was doing; mainly because I was burning the candle at both ends, catch what I mean? I was sure glad that nobody was in the elevator with me when that happened, but people all over the building heard the elevator crash into the basement floor. And it was the talk of the building; talk about embarrassing! No one said anything to me about the incident, but I got a pink slip the next payday. It was highly unusual for me to have that job anyway, in those days most elevator operators were white.

After I lost that job, I delivered bread for a local bakery. I took the bread to delivery stations in the neighborhoods in my red Express Wagon. When I came to San Marcos, I noticed that the Simon Bakery in town sold some of the same kind of breads.

Every chance I got I would go down to the wharf and get fish, mostly herring, off the trucks that would come in loaded up with herring to sell in the city. Even after they sold it, there would be some fish left over. You know because a fish can be a stinky thing, sometimes the fish merchants would hire us to help clean the fish boats. We would get paid in fish. Even at a young age I felt the responsibility to do whatever I could do to help put food on the table at home. Living in the city was very expensive; some things never change.

It was not long before Mother decided to take us back to Hume where living expenses would be much lower. While we were in Washington my grandfather's house was pretty much stripped and left in disrepair, since Harriet Thompson Washington, his second wife, took sick and moved in with her daughter, Margaret. A lot of my Granddad's furniture was gone, but I believe all the bedrooms still had beds in them. So we could not move in to his house until we fixed it up. In the meanwhile we stayed with Aunt Lucy for about six or seven months. Aunt Lucy's husband, Uncle Neely died around the time that we went back to Hume. It was at his funeral that my Aunt Lucy said that she didn't want to live in the house by herself, although she had her son, Robert Louis there. Well, she invited my mother and us children to move in with her and Robert. She lived about two miles from my grandfather's farm.

* * *

I felt I was a man; about seventeen or eighteen years old, I could do it all. The shingle roof leaked. So, we took the shingles off. Wilbur Green, a colored man, had opened a store in Hume. Wilbur bought several rolls of tin and delivered them to the house. My uncle Willie who was living in Harrisburg, Pennsylvania, had written a letter to Wilbur, asking him to find someone to fix the roof. Uncle Willie told Wilbur, "I know that boy [me] don't know how to put on that tin roof. You see to it that the roof work is done right." I got Mr. Putman, a tinner, to help me put on the roof. There was not much that I couldn't do if I put my mind to it!

Once the roof was fixed we still had some serious problems preventing us from moving back to the house. The old stove was in a real bad shape. Behind the firebox on the old stove, there was a tank about three feet long and about a foot deep where water was heated for baths and so forth. The new, coal-burning stove didn't have the water tank. I went to Paul Pierce's store in Markham, Virginia and bought my mother a brand new stove. I worked and paid for that stove and felt so proud that I could do this for her. Paul Pierce's store was located on Highway 55 where the railroad went through. Markham was seven miles from Hume. Like I said before, we had three general merchandise stores in town, but no hardware stores. West Poe had a store, but Wilbur Green bought his store. Charlie Cordor and Henry Paine also had small stores. Roy Wright bought Paine's store. Their stores sold canned goods, dry goods, and small hardware items such as nails and hand tools.

* * *

Some would say we were poor because we had very little money for food, and we didn't have Grandfather's vegetable garden or his hogs and chickens to supply our needs. We never felt that way because when food was low, and my mother would say, "Children, I don't know what we going to eat for dinner," one of us children would go out and catch a rabbit. Now let me tell you that was some kinda fun! We didn't see it as some difficult task because two or three of us children can make enough noise to cause the rabbit to run right to you. I saw my mother take one cottontail rabbit and feed all eight or nine of us; we had Aunt Carrie's four children, too. She would put that rabbit in a pot of water and cook it until it was almost done. Then she would pick all the bones out of the pot, and she would pour the corn meal in real slow, stirring until the corn meal was stiff. We could dip out the rabbit and meal and eat it with a fork. We'd all have rabbit so no one could fuss over who got this piece or that piece it all looked the same.

In the spring of the year, we would gather watercress, and you talk about something good, it was very delicious. When you had a rabbit cooked in the meal and cress or turnip greens, cabbage, mustard greens now that was good eating! I haven't seen watercress since I left Virginia. The watercress in Texas is different from the cress we had in the hills of Virginia. We would take a knife and cut it off right close to the ground. Somehow, we always managed to get three meals every day.

My grandfather's horses and equipment were all gone too, so I didn't do any farming on our farm when we returned to Hume. I went to work for different farmers, stacking their wheat straw or whatever I had to do to make a living. I never was one to take handouts and yet I liked to have what I needed; I even cleaned wells to help support my mother and siblings. I also worked during the harvest season ricking straw. When there was snow on the ground, farmers fed their livestock straw. The straw was stacked in one big pile so that the water would run out of it. The middle was kept higher, so the water wouldn't run in but out. A rick of straw would be approximately 12 to 15 feet high and 10 to 30 feet long. The straw was left over from the threshing of wheat, rye, barley, and oats. Oats were harvested early in the spring, Wheat was ready in June or July, and barley was harvested in the fall. So, threshing could take place two or three times a year, and the ricking followed the threshing. No tractors were used. Oxen were going out of favor. Horses were preferred to mules. But not everybody could handle a mule. I learned to rick straw and followed the threshing machine wherever crops were planted. I didn't ask the farmer if he wanted his straw ricked; I just got out there and did it. And when he paid the man with the threshing machine, he would pay me for doing the ricking. I didn't set a price. The length of the job varied; sometimes it took as long as two or three days to complete the ricking on a particular farm. It depended on the size of the farm. Sometimes, it didn't take but two or three hours if the farm was small. The straw had to be hauled to the thresher. Some farmers had two or three wagons. They would throw the load into the thresher. The thresher would go from farm to farm. Doing this work I earned the nickname 'Stack.'

* * *

We lived in Hume a few years (four or five years) without my stepfather, James, Molly and William's father. Dr. Goldenburg, a doctor in D. C., told him "James, the day you go back to work will be the day you die." He was working as a chef at the Raleigh Hotel in D.C. and my stepfather wasn't in any shape to work. He stayed fat; he was a big man, but he wasn't as tall as I am. He had to lose a lot of weight. Eventually, he made up his mind to come live with us in Hume. Right after he arrived, (he hadn't been there but a few months), my mother got a letter from my aunt Carrie who lived in Sharron's Hill, a suburb of Philadelphia, telling her that my aunt was sick. Her husband had died a short time prior to my mother's arrival in Philadelphia. My mother rushed on up there to see about her sister. She had been pregnant with Eloise when her husband died. So mother stayed on to help her. My aunt lived about a month more and she died. After the funeral, mother had to stay there to dispose of the property. My aunt's husband had been a carpenter and he had built their home. Mother had to sell the house and other property and bring the children, and there were four of them, Norman, Hezekiah, Albert, and Eloise back to Hume. Aunt Carrie was mother's baby sister. Fortunately, my stepfather was there to look after the house and children, while mother was in Philadelphia. I was at Grandfather's house then. I was about 18 or 20 years old at that time; it was somewhere around 1932 or 1933 and I was the breadwinner.

One day I came home and my stepfather told me he wanted some money; I gave him some, but not as much as he wanted. We had a falling out over that incident. I wasn't going to stay there and fuss with him. After the disagreement with my stepfather, I went to live with Frank Cook. Frank's wife had left him, and he didn't have anybody to take care of his children. He was working on the farm, so I took care of Frank's children. I didn't get any pay but had room and board. I would get up and fix breakfast for the children. I stayed there about two months. My mother wrote me a letter from Philadelphia PA in which she told me to go back home, but it took the letter a good week to reach me. Mother always could handle me. If I was doing something out of order and my mother would have a kind of jerk of her head and a certain look at me; I knew what that meant.

Mother's letter shook me up, and so I went back home. That was the only friction that I had with my stepfather. He was really a lovable man.

Mother came back and brought her sister's children, and so I went to work for Mr. Tom Kines to help support the family. I did odd jobs for him and his family. Mr. Kines was farming on land leased from the Stribling family. One of my responsibilities was to cut wood for the stove. The children looked up to me like a big brother. Out of the four of them only the youngest is still living today.

* * *

I had begun to notice that Mr. French Poles paid a lot of attention to me at church and other places in the community; I just thought he was being nice. Then my mother told me who he was; he was my father. I believe I had been doing some work for Mr. Poles when my mother said, "I want you to know that's your father." That's the way she told me. She said, "That's your father." Then I began to understand why he had been paying so much attention to me. I didn't let him know that I knew he was my father until some years later. I went to live with my mother in D.C. after my grandfather died. Then when she brought us back to Hume to live, I met my father again and let him know that mother had told me who he was. I think I was 15 or 16 years old at that time.

I worked on my father's farm about two years after I came back to Hume. Daddy owned several large tracts of farmland. He was a smart, industrious man who knew how to make money. He hired Russell Whitmore, Hezekiah Pennington, and Robert Poles, his nephew to work on his farm, but he would leave me in charge when he had to be away. Even though I was a teenager, the hired hands knew that my father had confidence in me to see that the work was done the way he wanted it done.

One day Daddy left us (Russell, Bob, Hezekiah, me, and a white man) in the field working. When Daddy returned, he came to the field where we were working shucking corn. The white man looked up and saw Daddy coming and started toward him trying to tell him something about the work. Daddy never looked at him or answered him. He just kept on walking until he got to where I was working. He walked up to me and asked, "Son, what's happening?" By his action, Daddy let the white man know that he wanted to hear what I had to say before he listened to his complaints. This incident made a deep impression on me because it demonstrated the kind of relationship that I had with my Daddy. He trusted me and respected my good judgment. Daddy's other children never knew how close we were. Daddy never gave me a nickel in his life, but he paid me whatever the other hands were earning. He taught me the importance of working to support myself.

I heard later that Robert and Hezekiah ran off with a traveling show that came to town. I don't know what made those boys want to work in that show. Daddy was away buying livestock when the boys ran off. When he came home and found out that the boys were gone, he did some checking to find out where the show would be next. He went to the show to bring the boys home. He located Bob, but Hezekiah Pennington had moved on with another part of the show. I don't know what happened to him. I was not working for Daddy at the time the boys ran off. Daddy brought Bob back, but I never heard from Hezekiah again.

I quit working for Daddy because his wife was jealous of me. She let Daddy know that she wasn't pleased with me being there. I lived in the house with him and his family while I was working for Daddy. I don't think she knew, but I overheard her making negative statements about me to Daddy. At that time, Daddy's oldest children were all girls, and that meant he spent more time with me than he did with them. In my mind at the time I thought this was what made his wife jealous. So, to keep from causing trouble for Daddy, I just quit and found myself another job. It was about 1929 and Daddy had bought a new '29 Ford. He said, "I am going to get Emily and bring her home." By the time he got back to the house I had packed and moved on. I wasn't going to be the cause of her leaving him again!

My daddy would see me in town and call me aside to give me advice on farm work and on how to live. He always gave me good advice. I could depend on his counsel. He gave more valuable instruction than anyone else knew because we never made a public issue of our personal relationship. I can remember returning to Virginia to visit my Daddy in 1984 when he was over ninety years old; he was nearly blind, but he could still get around and work his farm. He was in the barn milking a cow. I told him how much I learned from him when I was a young man. He said, "You know, I'm glad to hear that. I want you to go up to the house and tell them." I went by his house and told several of his children about the counseling that he had given me when I was a teenager. He wanted them to know about our close relationship. Nobody knew that Daddy cared as much for me as he did. I had lots of kin but I sure did miss knowing my brothers and sisters on my father's side.

* * *

My father was also a stock trader. He would come by and pick me up on his way to buy cattle at the stockyard and resell them. I used to drive the cows home from the stockyard for him. He would be riding along behind me in his brand new 1929 Ford. Sometimes, he would sell the cows before we got home. Somebody along the road would say, "French, how much you want for them cattle?" Daddy would ask, "How much you want to give me?" If the price were right, he would say to me, "Boy, turn them cattle into this man's lot." He would collect his money and go right back to the stockyard and buy some more cows. Daddy would always tell me "keep your money turning over. Don't just hold onto it." Then he would take me home to my mother, who lived in Grandfather's house. I would go with him to help him do whatever he wanted me to do. I loved being with him and learning from him.

Daddy also bought cattle for Mr. Bradshaw, who lived in Pittsburgh, Pennsylvania. On one occasion, Daddy bought $55,000.00 worth of cattle for Mr. Bradshaw at auction in Virginia. He wrote a check for the $55,000.00, but he had only about $1,800.00 in the bank. Back in those days, checks didn't move through the banks as quickly as they do today. As soon as the seller left the office, Daddy called Mr. Bradshaw and told him what he had done. Mr. Bradshaw called his banker and asked him to deposit $55,000.00 in French Poles' checking account in Marshall,

Virginia. Daddy wasn't worried about having the money in the bank when he made deals; he knew Bradshaw would cover any checks he wrote on his behalf. See, Bradshaw trusted Daddy to select the best cattle in the lot. Daddy was a good judge of cattle.

I liked the way my father conducted his business when he was buying livestock from sellers. He would ask the seller how much he wanted for the livestock. He would always tell the seller, "That's your livestock. I am not going to put a price on your cattle." Then the seller would have to name a price. If the suggested price was more than Daddy wanted to pay, he would say, "Well, I just don't think I can make that price." He wouldn't haggle or bargain with the seller for a lower price. Most sellers would then say to Daddy, "Well, what would you give me for these cows?" Daddy would make an offer, but if the seller asked him to raise the price, Daddy would just terminate the discussion. He was not there to argue over prices. He had a reputation for being a straightforward, no nonsense livestock buyer.

Sometimes, Mr. Bradshaw would not bring the livestock to market immediately. He would tell Daddy to feed the cattle for three or four months until he was ready to bring them to Pittsburgh to resell them. Daddy would make some extra money feeding the cattle until Mr. Bradshaw told him to ship the cattle by railroad. Daddy would not let the cattle lose weight while they were waiting to be sent to Mr. Bradshaw.

My father and I became very close during the time I worked for him. And we remained close throughout the rest of his life. The very last time I saw him, he was driving a tractor on his farm. He was about 94 years old.

Elder James Burrell
Pastor—Shiloh, Winchester, Va.
Pastor—Swift Ford, Criglersville, Va.

I learned a lot about life and about business from my father. Before he died, Daddy donated a large sum of money to his church, Beulah Baptist Church in Markham, Virginia for the restoration of the building, which had fallen into disrepair. He died on December 28, 1986 at age 96. My brother, Reverend James Burrell, who lived in Manassas, VA at the time, called to tell me my father had died.

CHAPTER 5

"The Ku Klux Clan make themselves known."

*

DURING THE EARLY to mid twenties, Fauquier County was a rough time to be alive and be black, catch what I mean? I wasn't too young to know what was going on. If I didn't see it for myself, I heard about it just listening to all the adult men talking. Charlie Cordor was a white man, who owned a store run by his brother-in law Jim Priest; he also owned the telephone company. The Post Office was in his store. Charlie was one of the most powerful men in the village. There was a lot of talk going around about his sister and a black man by the name of Jim Jordan. These two were involved in an unacceptable relationship for the time. Things escalated surrounding the bi-racial couple. Jordan got wind that something was about to happen to him and he quickly left the village. Sometime later, Charlie's sister left and nobody knew where either one of them had gone. Some years later Jim Jordan's mother became seriously ill and the news of her illness reached many newspapers. A letter came to the Post Office in Hume addressed to Jordan's mother. Most everyone figured Jim Priest opened the letter. He learned from the letter that Jordan was coming in on the train to Markham.

When the white folks got word about Jim's letter, they formed a posse and when he got off the train, a lynch mob was waiting for him. They lassoed Jim, tied the rope to an old Ford automobile and they dragged him to his death. Now there was a hearing about this type of lynching regarding Jordan. The judge made it plain that Jim Jordan would not be the only one to die with his boots on. At this point no one really knew who the Klan members were. Although this proved to be right; for a number of men later would die with their boots on, too. Old man Newton died with his boots on; Mr. Cable died with his boots on; Mr. Kerns went to the front of his car to crank it, but he dropped dead right there with his wife sitting in the car. There were many others including three of the Marshalls, a big name in the area. In those days Ku Kluxers were really bad in that part of the country. All those white men died with their boots on and were thought to have been involved in Jordan's death. In those days, when a black man got mixed up with a white woman, his life was always in danger.

Another black man named George Shepherd almost lost his life because of a white woman. George was a married man who got involved with a white woman. He had a car and drove over to her house. As he went through the gate to her house, he had to stop and fasten the gate. Knowing this, some Klan members hid at the gate in an attempt to catch him one night as he left. Somebody moved too quickly, and George realized what was about to happen. The Ku Kluxers were waiting for him to get out of his car to open the gate, but George just ran right through that gate with his car. The Klansmen followed him all the way home on horseback. When George got home, he ran in the house and hollered to his wife, "Birdie, open the door!" He ran in and locked the door behind him. He went upstairs where there was a knothole in the wall that allowed him to see outside without being seen. As the white men rode up on their horses wearing their Klan hoods and robes, George shot five or six of them and killed three. The scared Klan members left, giving George an opportunity to escape. They came back the next morning and searched George's house, but they never found him. The whole town knew the identities of the three Klansmen that George shot that night.

Shadrack Thompson was not as lucky as George Shepherd. This happened about 10-12 years later, in 1932. From the talk in the household where I worked, I recall it being said that Shad had been working for a white man named Mr. Henry Baxley, who owed Shad a lot of back wages. Baxley couldn't pay him because he was losing money on his farm. One night in February, Shad came back to the Baxley's and let himself in the house. He caught Mr. Baxley and his wife in the bed sleeping with their baby in an adjoining room. After knocking Baxley unconscious, Shad took Baxley's wife off into the woods behind Shad's parent's house. He kept Mrs. Baxley the rest of the night and sexually assaulted her to get back at her husband for refusing to pay him. Day was breaking next morning, when Mrs. Baxley came out of the woods. She went straight to Shad's parents' house and told them what had happened. Shad's mother was in the backyard when she saw Mrs. Baxley coming out of the woods wearing a nightgown. When Mr. Baxley regained consciousness, he took their little baby and drove to the Newton's, his wife's mother's house. The incident was reported to the sheriff and a search for Shad was started. He was hiding in the Rattle Snake Mountains. The white men got a posse together right quick to search for Shad and then disbanded after not finding him in 2 months. His body was found about 4 months later around June of the same year. Shad's body was discovered in the woods, and the sheriff was notified. But shortly before the Sheriff arrived, somebody threw a match on the body and burned it up. It had been soaked with gasoline. Mrs. Baxley stayed with the Newton's, and her husband came to live there also. Like I said, I was working for the Newton's when Shad was killed, and white people did whatever they wanted to do to black folks back in those days.

* * *

As a teenager working for the Newton family in Hume, I took Mr. Baxley's truck once and drove up in the hills to get a load of firewood. As I said, Mr. Baxley and his wife were living on the Newton farm. Mrs. Baxley was Mrs. Newton's daughter. Nobody had told me to take the truck and gather wood. You see, I had never driven any kind of motor vehicle before. But the truck was sitting there with the keys in it. I noticed that we were nearly out of firewood, and I knew the workers had sawed up a fresh supply and stacked it up in the woods. So, I decided to go up the mountain and bring back some firewood. Nobody ever showed me how to shift the gears; I just experimented until I found the right gears to go forward and backwards. It was a big flat bed truck with five or six gears for going forward. I got the load of wood and came back down the mountain. When I got back to the house, I had to back the truck up to the basement where the wood was kept. But that's where I ran into some trouble. I didn't know how to back up. The Newton's kept hearing the truck running with me trying to back up, so they sent Baxley out to see what was going on. Mr. and Mrs. Newton didn't fuss at me at all; they knew I was just trying to help. But Baxley did tell me not to drive the truck again. I really didn't know what I was doing. I might have driven in low gear or some gear all the way up the mountain and back. I wanted to see what it would be like to drive that truck. I have always been curious about things, and I was never scared to try something new.

CHAPTER 6

"I was making big money now; Tom Kines paid me $11.00 a month."

*

I GOT A job on Tom Kines' farm sometime in the early 1930's. Mr. Kines leased or rented farmland from the Stribling family. Like most farmers in Fauquier County he raised corn, wheat, rye, oats, and other grains. After the grains had been sifted, Mr. Kines selected the best seeds for planting the next season. Because Mr. Kines suffered seriously with lumbago, I had to feed the animals, do the plowing, and milk the cows, take care of the sheep and lambs. I did all that work for $11.00 per month. I made more money on that job than I had ever earned before. On the 3rd of January, I had $132.00 in my bank account. So, if you figure this out you see that $11.00 x 12 months equal $132.00, which was my salary for the entire year. I mention this because this figure occurred many times throughout my life and was significant each time but for different reasons. While $132 was my annual salary, it was not how I got that money in the bank. Even though working for Mr. Kines, I got my meals free and I could eat three meals a day. My mother received 20 bushels of meal. Mr. Kines allowed me to get a gallon of milk every day or a cow. I decided to take the cow and leave it with my mother. Mother also got a barrel of flour. Additionally, as part of my wages, Mr. Kines allowed me to get so many pounds of butchered hog meat or a hog to feed and butcher for ourselves. We took the hog. Everybody who worked on farms got the same arrangement—a little money and some payment in farm produce.

Now I lived on the farm with the Kines Family but my room had a separate entrance. I could come and go without disturbing them. I ate in the same dining room with the Kines family, but not at the same table. I ate my meals at a table set off to the side of the room, and they ate at the big dining room table. But they served me the same food that they ate.

I remember an incident that really scared me. Mr. and Mrs. Kines had one daughter named Margie. She was a smart little girl, but she was bad. I had made it a habit of doing whatever she asked me to do. But one day, she asked me to do something while I was busy chopping wood for the stove. Nobody told me what needed to be done. If something had to be done, I did it. We needed wood, so I was cutting some. I told Margie I would do what she wanted me to do later, but she wanted me to do it right then. I just ignored her and continued cutting the wood. She picked up a chip of wood, said something to me, which caused me to turn toward her. At that moment she threw the chip and struck me right square in the eye. Bam! Oh! That hurt! And she stood there grinning. Before I knew it, I had slapped that girl, and knocked her to the ground. She got up and went inside but she didn't cry until she got in the house. Her mother and father grabbed her and asked "What's the matter?" She told them that I had hit her. They ran out of the house to confront me. By that time my eye was swollen shut and blood running down my face. They could see what happened. I told them she had thrown a chip and hit me in the eye. I was scared because at that time black people were often lynched for hitting a white person. But Mr. and Mrs. Kines didn't bother me at all; in fact, Mrs. Kines washed my eye with boric acid. I had to wear a patch over that eye for a while. The Kines were just good people.

Now of course, out of my salary I needed some money for my personal things, like shaving cream and tooth paste, etc. So it might help to know that while I was working for Mr. Kines, I bought a hog for $10.00 from a man who needed the money in a hurry. I don't think he knew the sow had already been bred. I didn't know that either. I just turned the hog loose with Mr. Kines' hogs. That hog later gave birth to eight pigs. I sold the pigs and made $132.00. That's how I got the $132.00 to put in the bank. But it is not the last time you will see this number!

CHAPTER 7

"Elizabeth Ambler and Sandlot Baseball on Sunday caused me concern!"

*

AUNT LUCY WASHINGTON, my cousin Robert's mother and some other ladies were serving a dinner for the Amblers and learned that they needed a houseboy. They came by and told my mother about it and she sent me over to the Amblers to apply for the work. At the same time Mary Moore from Orlean had been hired as a cook. While Mary didn't stay long, I worked as a houseboy and helped with the cooking for the Ned Ambler family in the early 1930's for about 30 months. I started this job in the spring.

The Amblers were good people and they were prominent people in the area. Jim, who was Ned Ambler's oldest son, was superintendent of schools, and his father was president of a bank in Warrenton, Virginia. They had three homes, one in Florida, the place in Hume Virginia, and another in Atlantic City, New Jersey. They lived up and down the east coast wherever they wanted, depending on the weather. The Hume farm consisted of approximately 27 hundred acres; it was a big farm. They also owned wild horses and I rode and broke horses for the Amblers. I'd just go out there and get me a horse and break him and ride him. Old man Ambler had a rule, if you broke a horse for him; you could break one for yourself. He would just give you that horse that you broke.

The Amblers had a main house and two other houses on the place. The foreman lived in a house right down the hill from the main house. There was a house for the workers also. There was a road that went from Route 688 to the Amblers Farm and beyond to Route 647, the road from Marshall to Crest Hill. It was a mile from 688 to the house and just under a mile from the house to 647. The foreman lived in the house on the road from the Amblers house to 688. The other house was between the Amblers and 647. I stayed in the big house with the Amblers and Mary did too. My room was up over the kitchen, which was built off the back part of the house. It had a breezeway from the kitchen to the dining room. Mary's bedroom was upstairs over the dining room and accessed by back stairs that went up from the hallway. The hallway was between the dining room and another room. An average day for me began around 6 AM, and I would get up and milk the cows and bring the milk to the house; then after feeding the chickens, I would turn them out into the yard. I would then start the fire in the kitchen stove for Mary to cook. The old man was already up and out riding the fences before we got up. The rest of the house slept while we busied ourselves with preparing the breakfast. Breakfast always started when Mr. Ambler came back from riding. This was where the real job began . . . you see they all wanted eggs and all wanted them fixed different.

Now the Amblers had four children, Edward (who died before I started working for them), Ann (who was married and living in Fairfax, VA), Jim (who was living in Warrenton VA but came home often) and Elizabeth (who was away at William and Mary College). Jim lived in Warrenton where his office was; he was the Superintendent of Schools. A short period of time after I started working for the Amblers, Elizabeth Ambler came home from college for the summer. Living way back on the farm the way they did, her mother sent me out with her wherever she went. She and her mother were the only ones who could drive the one car they had. Mr. Ambler could not drive but he sure could ride a horse. They drove him to work every day. Elizabeth was real playful whether I was working or not. She and I were about the same age.

From time to time my father would see me in town in Elizabeth's car. My daddy got kind of uneasy about me riding around with the Amblers' daughter. He was scared that the whites on the farm would get jealous of me. You see, I had free access to the Amblers' home, front door, back door, upstairs, downstairs; I roamed the place without restrictions. I carried Charlie Roberts, the Amblers' gardener, right in the front door to speak to the Amblers. I would just use the closest door; it didn't make any difference. The white hands couldn't do that—walk all over the house like I could. See, they had to go to the back door. This is what my father thought was going to stir up a mess and cause a big ruckus—because of my being black and this was a very prejudiced town at that time.

* * *

    While I was working for the Amblers, I was struck by lightning. The Amblers were in Atlantic City at the time. I was left to look after the place in their absence. Since my room was above the kitchen, part of the chimney from the cook's stove went right up the wall. Part of my job was to help Charlie Roberts, the gardener, with his work since I was not needed in the main house. A storm came up while we were working in the garden. I told Charlie, "Come on, go to the house with me." We went upstairs to my room. I was lying across my bed and Charlie was sitting in a chair. I got up and opened the window to get some fresh air because it was hot in the room. Charlie said, "You ought not to open that window; the lightning will come in." I said something smart like, "The lightning can come down through the top of the house as well as anywhere else." A few minutes later, while I was lying on the bed, I heard a boom, and the next thing I knew, when I came to, I was stone blind." I got up and couldn't see. Charlie thought I was dead and had gone down stairs; but when he heard me walking around he came back up to my room. He walked in there and hugged me and said, "Man, I thought you were dead." I told him I could not see! He said, "The storm is over now; I'll take you home." We walked from the Amblers' home to my mother's house across the fields straight to the house. I couldn't see anything. I stayed at home about two days and my sight began to return. My mother always believed my sight would return quickly. Mother would wash my eyes with boric acid every day. Amazingly I had no burns from the lightning. In fact, the lightning had split the brick chimney in my room from top to bottom. You could stick your hand sideways in the space left by the split. Charlie fed the chickens and the farm hands milked the cows while I was at home recovering. I went back to work after regaining my sight.

    Some of my other duties at the Amblers' included gathering the eggs, manicuring the yard and working the flower beds; sometimes I would help the cook peel potatoes, etc. Mrs. Ambler could find something for you to do every second of the day. I was the only black person working for the Amblers at that time. All the other hands were white, except Charlie Roberts, the gardener and Mary Moore the cook. But Charlie didn't live there.

* * *

Now Elizabeth was a slender, playful, pretty blond-haired girl, about 5'8" tall. I'd be sitting down at the table, and Elizabeth would walk in and sit right down in my lap, and her mother would be in the kitchen with us. They didn't have the prejudice that the other whites had. And Elizabeth would play round with me; if I had finished my work, we would go to town. Most black folks would have to sit in the back seat when they were riding with white folks, but I would be in the front seat with Elizabeth.

My father got so nervous about it that he kept going to my mother, telling her to get me to quit that job. There were already two or three lynchings in Fauquier County, but the Amblers were not involved. Nevertheless, my father was afraid there was going to be a lynching because of Elizabeth's playfulness with me. I began to understand my father's concern when Elizabeth and I were left alone in the house one day. Elizabeth's mother had driven her father to the bank one morning. She told me before she left that her daughter was sick and for me to get her whatever she needed. Elizabeth was upstairs in her room, and I was downstairs doing my work. Well, her mother and Mr. Ned hadn't been gone thirty minutes before Elizabeth called me. She said, "Bring me some hot water up here." I carried the water to her. She said, "Put the basin over there on the stand." When I turned around, she had fastened the door. She said "You know that book, *Black Beauty*, that you have been wanting, I got it from the library." And I said, "Good!" I was excited about reading *Black Beauty*. But she told me I would have to read it in her room. At first, I thought she was concerned about Mrs. Ambler catching me reading downstairs when I was supposed to be working. So, I picked the book up and began reading. She got up out of her bed and sat down beside me. When she did that, I thought of my father's warning about my being caught with a white girl.

Elizabeth's playfulness got so bold that I decided to talk to her about it. I brought up my concerns about lynchings, and she said, "Alphonso!" she was the only one in the house who called me Alphonso. Her mother called me Al; her father called me Bill all the time and I don't know where he got the name Bill. Elizabeth said, "Alphonso, that'll never happen, (referring to lynching). My daddy thinks too much of me to low-grade me in a scandal like that. My parents wouldn't do that. And even if it did happen, if you and I did get together and got caught at it—they would send you away or they would send me away, but it would not be a public scandal." Now, those were the words she spoke to me. But I was thinking about what would happen to me if the white folks caught Elizabeth and me away from the house where her father couldn't protect us. She never thought about that. I knew her life would not be in danger, but I could have been lynched before Mr. Ambler ever got the news. My father was so worried nevertheless about me because of what happened to a local black man.

The fate of the local young black man who had a baby by one of the white women in town was very disturbing to me. He was lynched by a posse formed by a foreman from one of the big farms. The young man found out that the mob was coming to get him and tried to escape, but they caught him in a cornfield and lynched him. The girl he had the baby with told her father that she wanted the boy to stay and see his child. By then her daddy had talked too much and folks in the town heard about the relationship. Then her father couldn't stop the lynch mob that caught the boy. When the black people in Hume heard about the lynch mob, the young man was already dead. He was somewhat older than me, and I was eighteen or nineteen years old at that time.

The girl vanished after the boy was lynched. Her people lost her as a result of that incident. She begged her father not to lynch him. Her family was middle class white; her daddy was foreman of a farm. Elizabeth had said, "Only poor white trash would make a public scandal about a white woman and a black man being intimate." But I realized that once word of a black man having a relationship with a white woman became public knowledge, the lynch mob would form and it couldn't be stopped. No one could control a lynch mob. In a case like the lynching of that boy, the black community couldn't go to the law for justice because the law was the worst place to go in a case like that. The law set up the lynching in the first place.

My father's concern for my safety finally moved me to quit. So, I waited for an excuse to quit. One day Mrs. Ambler stepped too close to a rake and one of the prongs penetrated the side of her shoe, not the sole of the shoe. I heard her hollering and found her on the ground where she fell. I pulled the prong out of her foot. Mrs. Ambler had a hot temper, and she blew up at me about leaving the rake in the yard. She said a lot of things she should not have said. I used that incident as a reason to quit. Mrs. Ambler came to my house after I quit trying to get me to return to work. She said, "Al, I thought you knew me better than that." I just told her I wasn't coming back to work.

You see, even after Elizabeth married, she would still catch me by myself doing my work and tickle me and play with me. She had married a lawyer, and I was concerned about his reaction to her playfulness. I didn't know what he would do if he happened to catch her playing with me. Why she played with me like that, I don't know. I didn't start it; she started it. But finally I got too concerned and left.

* * *

My next job was working for the Kines. This was a great time for me. Some of the young men in our neighborhood had started a sandlot baseball team. We didn't have uniforms. We were lucky to have baseballs, bats and gloves. My first cousin James "Jimbo" Poles was the manager/coach of our team. Gladys Washington's husband, Robert, was one of our catchers. We played black teams in our area. We never played against the white teams. At that time Satchel Paige, an upcoming famous Negro who would end up pitching for the Kansas City Monarchs, was our idol. Carroll Rector was our star player. Carroll was brother to the Rector Sisters who used to sing when I was preaching at different churches in Virginia in later years. Now listen, I saw that boy, Carroll squat on his knees behind the plate and catch that ball and put out a player on second base without ever rising to his feet! He would just dare a player to try to steal a base. He was some kind of catcher. I was somewhere around 18 and 19 at this time. My mother didn't like for me to play baseball on Sunday because she said, "Sunday is the Lord's Day." However, one Sunday, my cousin Robert was supposed to play, but didn't show up. I took his place in the line up. I played in the outfield. Somebody else did the catching in Robert's absence. I was playing right field and Emmett Baltimore was playing center field. A player hit a ball, and I ran to catch it, but Emmett was also running to it. I out ran Emmett and I went up and caught the ball, but on my way down, I collided with Emmett as he went up to get the ball. My chin hit Emmett's head and I was knocked out cold; but I held the ball, they say. I woke up the following Tuesday morning. My teammates had carried me to a woman we knew as Aunt Ginny. They didn't want to take me home because they knew my mother didn't approve of my playing ball on Sundays.

We played our games in the bottoms. Jimbo used his daddy's car to transport our team equipment, such as we had. He would hook a harrow to the car and break up the ground for the diamond. Then he would pull a heavy roller over the surface to make it smooth. The pitcher's mound was built up out of the dirt; there was a hole in the top of the mound where the pitcher would stick his toe. These were items supplied by the county. We bought our canvas bases. The bases had long spikes that were used to anchor them. The bats we used were called "The Louisville Slugger." We played every week and our season lasted as long as the weather was good. We would also travel to communities like Cresthill, Flint Hill, Orlean, or Markham to play. All the little towns in that area had a baseball team.

Segregation prevented us from playing the white teams, but we could go watch their teams play, and they would come to our games also. We played Saturday or Sunday but never both days so we could go to the other games. We didn't have stands or bleachers like they have now. But the white high school in Hume had bleachers, and the white baseball teams often played at the school. The white boys had some good teams in Hume.

CHAPTER 8

"I found out the identity of several local Klan members."

*

THE MILLARD BIRDSALL Dairy needed help. I found out before I moved to Loudoun County in 1934. I suppose I was about 21-22 years old at the time when Henry Cook came up to the house in Hume, looking for somebody to go to work with him at Birdsall's Dairy. He worked the farm for Alfred Dueling in Waterford VA but he was leaving him to go to work for Birdsall the next year. Well, I wasn't working then so I went with Henry to see about the job. This would have been around the last of August or first part of September. Henry and I both got jobs. Back then the workers usually moved from one farm to another in December because the work year started around the first of January.

Mr. Birdsall actually was selling bottled milk to the folks in town, house to house. He had lots of customers. Birdsall would drive the milk truck and I would deliver the milk to the customer's door. While at the door I would pick up the empty milk bottles to be carried back to the Dairy and washed and refilled. Mr. Birdsall had a machine for capping the milk. Now these caps were pasteboard caps and if one dropped it had to be thrown out. Eventually, he had to quit delivering milk this way because of the state laws. The state got very strict about keeping the bottles clean and way you keep the barn. The Delaval Company supplied him with the latest machinery to milk the cows. He already had the Delaval separators. He sold milk and butter and cream in town back then. In order to comply with the new state laws, if he was going to stay in this milk business, he built a new barn, bought more cows and used new equipment from the DeLaval Milking Machines Products. DeLaval began making these in 1878 after Gustaf de Laval who was born in 1845 and died the year I was born, 1913, patented the cream separator that revolutionized dairy production. He had a will to improve not only machines, but the very conditions of living.

He firmly believed that it is possible to make a difference. It was about 1934 that DeLaval came up with the first milking parlor machines.

These machines had flow control milking. The milk came out of the cow, into the bucket, from the bucket it was carried to the cooler, from the cooler into the ten-gallon milk can. When it came out of the cooler it was cold! He began selling the milk wholesale in ten-gallon cans. Selling milk directly to customers made them the ones to worry about the state laws that dairies had to obey or observe. The big truck that would come to pick up the milk stopped where the dirt road ended at the highway. They would not come onto a dirt road or your driveway . . . they stayed on the county or state road only. I had to carry that milk from the dairy farm up to a main hard surface road. Sometimes I left the milk in the milk stands there by the highway. The Birdsall farm was about a mile from the hard surface road. Birdsall shipped about seven or eight cans every day. Henry and I did the morning milking at around 4:00 and in the evening Birdsall and I did the milking unless I had to do it all by myself.

At the same time the state changed and he made all these changes in his milking methods, Mr. Birdsall's mule died. His mule dying caused him to switch to tractors. He had more corn to grow because he had more cows and mules would not stand up to this work like the tractor. You could do more with one tractor than you could with 6 mules!

* * *

It was a real learning experience for me in more ways than I wanted to learn. But one of the concepts I have carried through my life to this day. For instance, in order to make cows produce milk on a regular basis, you have to milk a cow at the same time every day and at the same speed in order not to interrupt her milk producing cycle. You would also have to feed the cows according to the amount of milk they gave. There was a real system to milking cows, and having a system has always been my way to do anything, and this stuck with me throughout my life. But the other learning experience came when I learned that Millard Birdsall was a Ku Klux Klan member. It was after I had been working for him several years. Once I found out he was a Klan member, I finished out the year but never worked for him again. I didn't want to work for anyone in the Klan. Another man, a few dairy farms from Birdsall named Kirby was also a Klan member. My good friend Harry King worked for him, and he left also. We both hoped to never be involved with anyone in the Klan again!

CHAPTER 9

"Saved, Baptized, Preaching, Plumbing and Dancing, uh oh!"

*

A FEW YEARS before leaving Birdsall's Dairy Farm, I had become acquainted with a family of people in Lincoln VA next door to the Mt. Olive Baptist Church. The family was named Trammell, Amos Trammell. He had five children of his own who were mostly grown. He also raised a couple other children, his niece and nephew whose parents had died. These two were Detsy and Cliff Lee. They were all members of Mt. Olive. I became very fond of Detsy, who was a member of the Mt. Olive church choir. Detsy and I had made arrangements to go out this particular night. We didn't realize there was a revival going on at the church. I walked over to pick her up but she was next door at the church. That really upset me something terrible! I made a plan to get her out of the choir that night to be with me. But my plan was no match for her faith. She insisted that I go around to the front of the church and sit in there until after services were over. I went around to the front of the church and stepped inside taking a seat on one of the benches near the middle. I was so involved thinking about Detsy I didn't realize that the revival was underway until I walked into the sanctuary. The preacher's sermon hit me hard. It seemed every word he was saying was like driving nails in me. Now that evangelist was powerful and he began to preach and something began to work in me. I had been running from the call to preach for about nine years now even though I had never been baptized. When the doors to the church were opened by the evangelist for anyone to come forward two of us appeared at the front; Detsy's sister and I. How I ended up in the front of this church is a mystery to this day. I was baptized in Mt. Olive Baptist Church in Lincoln but never joined that church. I wanted to join Providence Missionary Baptist Church in Orlean VA near my home in Hume and had a good reason, too! However I worked and taught

Sunday school at Mt. Olive for some time and continued to see Detsy. Years later I would run into one of these children, an older woman then who remembered me teaching her in Sunday school there. She came to Hume for a homecoming service. You will catch that later on.

* * *

I had been a member of Providence Baptist Church for about one year when I became mysteriously ill while working for Mr. Birdsall. I became so ill I could not do anything for myself including getting back home to Hume for my mother to care for me. Mr. Birdsall carried me home to her in his car. He had taken me to two or three doctors in Purcellville because I was so weak that I could hardly walk. They could find nothing wrong with me. Prior to this time my mother had hoped I would join Mount Morris Baptist Church. But you see, I had witnessed the treatment that my grandfather received from other preachers in the Association of Primitive Baptists, so it was clear to me that I wasn't going through with that; I did not even answer my call to preach at first. Now, that I became ill I knew exactly what was happening; God was using my illness to get my attention and bring me to an acceptance of my calling. I had never told anybody about this experience of the call to preach. I understood my call, but I just refused to answer it. I thought I could do what I wanted to do without thinking about the greatness of God. The doctor was called, but he couldn't find anything wrong with me. My mother had to feed me; I fell out of the bed and couldn't get back in the bed. Mother got the other children to help put me back in bed. Somehow this mysterious illness moved me to accept my call to preach.

You see, nine years before this happened; I had been called to preach. The call came to me in a dream; I had been given a bushel of corn to plant; I was shown where to plant. While working with my grandfather, I had learned that a bushel of corn was supposed to plant five acres. I started to plant the five acres of corn; after I had finished planting the five acres, I looked and I still had a bushel of corn, and I still had five acres to plant. That disturbed me somewhat. I asked God about it. I had that dream maybe a year before my grandfather died.

Soon after I had been baptized at Mt. Olive, I learned that the pastor at Orleans was also the pastor at Round Hill, three miles from Purcellville. On the second Sunday of the month, he preached at Providence Missionary

Baptist Church in Orlean, and on the fourth Sunday, he was at Round Hill, about five miles from where I lived. Therefore, I lived close enough to Round Hill to attend services.

* * *

While I was sick and staying with my mother in Hume, my brother James Burrell and his wife, Pearl were living with her. Pearl was pregnant (a couple months) with their first child. My brother James did not belong to church and loved to party and dance every weekend. Pearl was a church-going woman. Between my mother and I we could not get him to stop drinking and dancing all around the area. I had been doing the same thing and probably started him on the same path, but I was changed now and tried to change him. We could not manage to do this but I'll tell you who did. I was home for about 2 or 3 months after my strength came back to me. One Friday evening James came home from work and Pearl had his bath water heated and his fancy clothes laid out as it was his custom to go to the dances on Friday night. He got dressed after eating his dinner and came out of the back room to the front by the stairs. Coming down the stairs was Pearl dressed to the nines in a shoulder-less, backless evening gown, hair all gussied up and makeup on—looking mighty fine. James took one look at her and said, "Where you going?" Pearl said, "With my husband." James stood there and looked at her a few moments before sighing and saying, "Pull that off." He turned around and went back to the room downstairs and pulled off his clothes. That was all it took to put a stop to his carrying on. Three little words, 'with my husband.' Shortly after that he was baptized and called to preach. He would later become the beloved pastor of Swift Ford Baptist Church in Crigglesville and another church in Winchester VA.

* * *

For a while I did a lot of preaching for local pastors when they were away from their churches for various reasons. I needed a way to get around and made a bargain with Randolph Rector, a friend, to carry me to my preaching engagements. One night I visited in their house and heard his sisters sing. I begged their mother to let them go with me to sing for me. Although we were in Loudon County at that time, the Rector Sisters were raised up between Hume and Marshall, Virginia. The three Rector Sisters had beautiful voices, and they were excellent singers. Their mother had trained them to sing. Her son, Randolph and the girls eventually persuaded her. The baby girl was a 10-year old named Gladys Rector. She became the lead singer for the group. I began to carry them everywhere I went. The Rector Sisters and one of their brothers were with me when I received the injury that left a large scar on my chin not to mention all my broken and chipped teeth. I had just finished preaching at Trough Hill Primitive Baptist Church in a place called Cresthill, Virginia. When I came out of the church, I started to crank the car. I think it was a Durant. Those old cars didn't have glass windows; they had curtains that would be snapped in place in case of rain or wind. My mother followed me out to the car; I attempted to crank the car while listening to what she was saying. Sometimes when you cranked those old cars, they would kick back if the spark was too far down. When I spun the cranking tool around, the starter kicked back, and the cranking tool flew out of my hand and hit me below my bottom lip, cutting a hole clean through the flesh. I was scheduled to preach that same night at Purcellville. Sometimes, I would preach four sermons in one day, going from church to church. I thought I could go on to Purcellville and preach, but the Rectors and my mother could see the seriousness of the injury, and they told me that I needed to see a doctor. We stopped in Marshall, about nine miles from Cresthill to find a doctor to treat my injury. While I was in the doctor's office, Brother Rector called ahead to the church in Purcellville and told them I wouldn't be able to preach due to an accident. The doctor sewed up the cut and sent me home. The anesthesia made my lips and part of my face numb, so I wasn't in any condition to preach. I could hardly talk, not to mention all my broken teeth!

* * *

Now I'm telling you, in that part of the country beginning preachers had a terrible time. The congregations did everything they could to try you and make you prove that you had been called. You catch what I mean? In the first six months or a year, the young preacher would experience situations in which he would have to overcome great difficulties. If you were going to fail, this would be the opportunity to fail. The congregations did all they could to try to make you fail. That really bothered me, too.

Later I became a trustee of a piece of land purchased for a Baptist church in Purcellville VA. We began the building and got the walls up when The War broke out. I'm talking about World War II. The County, saying that they were changing the street names in the area, contacted me. Later, (after I was living in TX) they were able to track me down and telling me I was the only trustee alive and something had to be done about the building; so I gave them my consent to do what they wanted.

* * *

After leaving Birdsall I needed a job and answered an ad in the paper for a plumber's helper. There were three of us who answered that ad and I was the only black. We were there before the gates opened. The man who opened the gate was Mr. T. J. Hatcher, the owner. He put the men to work who had come in and ignored the three of us until they had all left. He told us to go into the warehouse and bring everything down to the yard in separate piles and inventory them. He gave us a notebook and pencil to do this. Nothing was said about hiring or a salary for us but he just put us to work. We worked until noon when we stopped for lunch. After lunch one of the boys did not come back. That left two of us. We worked until quitting time that night which was after five. The next morning I went in to work but the other man did not show up. I worked until mid morning putting all the stuff back in the warehouse on the main floor. After I got it all in the warehouse I went to the office to see what else Mr. Hatcher wanted me to do. Hatcher said to me, "Sit down. I guess you noticed that I did not ask you where you worked or what you knew about plumbing. First of all, I don't need your reputation from anyone else because those people can lie as well as you. What I wanted to see was if you could follow orders. If so, I can teach you what you need to know." That evening I finished up what I was doing and cleaned up around the building until quitting time and went home. The next day Mr. Hatcher sent me out to work with a man named Dick Caesar, a black man who laid tiles for sewer drains. One day Dick became sick with lumbago and couldn't work. He was off work for quite a while. I began to work with a master plumber named Dutch Hogan. I became his assistant or a plumber's helper. Dutch was installing a pump in a well, but he couldn't get it to pump. He called the owner Mr. Hatcher and asked for help. Hatcher told him to reverse the wires. Dutch had been running the pump backwards. I became fascinated with Mr. Hatcher. He had five master plumbers working for him, and he owned about 15 plumbing trucks; I could tell that he loved plumbing, and he knew it very well. You see, without coming to the job site, Mr. Hatcher knew exactly how to solve the problem that Dutch was having with that water pump. From that experience, I learned a good plumber would need to know something about electricity. I also began to think about becoming a plumber myself; owning my own business.

Unbeknownst to Mr. Hatcher or Dutch, every night I would take one of Hatcher's plumbing books home and read it. I had a key to the building, so I could return the books first thing the next morning before either missed them. One day we were behind schedule on a job, so I asked Dutch if he wanted me to run some vents on a building nearby to help him catch up with the work. He said, "Don't let the inspector catch you." This was the first time I had a chance to use the skills I had picked up from reading Mr. Hatcher's plumbing books and watching Dutch do his job. I was busy installing vents and was so interested in what I was doing that I didn't notice anyone was around me. I was up on a ladder putting flashing where I had run the vent. Suddenly I heard somebody say, "Hey boy, come down here. I want to see your license." It was the inspector. He told me I had to leave the job because I didn't have a license. I returned to the shop and Mr. Hatcher wanted to know why I had left the job site. I told him what the inspector had said to me. Then Hatcher said, "You go on back to work. I'll take care of the inspector." I went back to the job site and continued installing the vents. That same inspector came back and caught me again. He said, "I thought I sent you back to the shop." I told him that Hatcher had sent me back. He said, "You tell Hatcher I'll see him in court." I went back and delivered the inspector's message to Hatcher. Monday morning I asked Hatcher what he wanted me to do. He told me to go back to work, and he would keep the inspector busy in the courthouse. That's how I got to learn plumbing work. I was on the job there for about a year and half.

We were working on the Lincolnia High School in Alexandria VA and had been there for some months. Mr. Hatcher came around to where we were working and asked us if anyone could lay tile. No one said anything so he left. Dick had been off and he needed someone to lay the tiles for him. He came back about half an hour later and repeated his question. Now after he left the first time, I got to thinking that since I was the last one hired, I might be the first one laid off after this job was finished if not before. So the second time he asked us, I told him I could do it. He told me to get two men and come with him. So this meant he put me in charge of two men! We went around to the other side and went to work... I was sure nervous about whether I was getting this done right or not... but soon the bulldozers were covering it up with dirt. The inspectors had passed the work and man, did I feel good. I felt like dancing!

* * *

Well, even being a preacher at this time, I still enjoyed running around to the dances and clubs in Washington DC if I got the chance. Now I didn't pass up a preaching engagement to go to a dance but if nothing was happening, watch out! I would be gone! Greyhound had a bus line that ran through Purcellville to Washington. I was on that bus as often as I could be. Not just me but that was how most of us got around then. Mostly I was interested in the big bands and big names of the times. I can remember going to hear a young Ella Fitzgerald who was from Southern Virginia. She had won the famous amateur night contest at the Apollo Theatre in Harlem in 1934. But she really got her start when Chick Webb, a drummer, heard her sing and invited her to perform with his band. They often came to Club Prudence in Washington DC. If I heard she was coming, I was there. I didn't let any grass grow under my feet. I wasn't there when *this* happened, but I heard that Ella was singing in a club and the pitch of her voice cracked the glasses on the tables. I was astonished to learn that a woman's voice could cause glasses to break.

The night Chick Webb died, Ella was leading his band. Chick was in Johns Hopkins Hospital in Baltimore. Ella was in Washington DC. I was in the dance club that night; it was June 16, 1939. The news of Chick's death came to her just as the band was about to come on the bandstand. Ella walked out on the stage and announced that she was going to sing a song entitled "My Buddy." But when she finished singing that song, there wasn't a dry eye in the place. Then she announced that Chick had died. Out of respect to Chick, the dance was cancelled. I also went to dances where Cab Calloway and his sister Blanche played. Blanche had her own band. I can remember Cab wearing his blue pinstripe zoot suit with rhinestone buttons and the long pocket chain. That was the style then. He would do his "Hi De Hi De Ho!" Dancing was my thing back then! I also heard the Duke Ellington band. In New Jersey, I went to hear Fats

Waller at a club one night, and he played "Who Dat Said Who Dat When I Said Who Dat?" That was one of his most popular numbers. He would be playing and he would say "Who dat"? And then an echo would repeat his words. Waller would then ask, "Who dat said 'who dat?' when I say 'who dat?'" I also remember seeing Hazel Scott, the boogie-woogie queen. She was a great piano player. She could take a church song and play it like a boogie-woogie. Of course, the church folks didn't like that at all. Hazel got involved with Adam Clayton Powell, Jr. and she helped a lot with his political career, raising money for his campaign and just supporting him in any way she could. Understandably, Powell's wife was uncomfortable with his involvement with Hazel. Consequently, Mrs. Powell caused a big disturbance in Abyssinian Baptist Church, where Powell was pastor. But eventually, Powell divorced his wife and married Hazel Scott. Besides Club Prudence, bands played at the Lincoln Colonnade and the Masonic Temple in D.C. It was at one of the dances in the Masonic Temple that a girl I was dancing with said to me, "You don't belong dancing here!" She turned and walked away from me . . . and that was the end of my dancing.

This had a profound influence on me because I knew that she was right. This part of my life was hard to let go. When she made that statement to me I almost could not wait for the bus to get there and take me home. Once back in Purcellville VA the news about this band or that just didn't appeal to me anymore.

* * *

The sudden death of T. J. Hatcher caught us all by surprise and brought about many changes in lots of lives. His wife sold the business and that split up the workers. From Hatcher's I went to work at Conwell's Slaughter House in Purcellville. He was in desperate need of workers because of the War. After I started with Conwell, he sold out the business to Armour & Company. Armour was contracted by the government to supply meat for the Armed Forces. We were required to slaughter 400 hogs a day! Each day we fell short then the Army took over the operation and sent a major to operate the business. No one was fired but the major then became the boss. My job was to remove the intestines. He called a plant meeting and told us we were going to work three 8-hour shifts 7 days a week! Sundays were busy days for me, being a preacher. Most of the workers in the slaughter house were black. The business workers were white. Before I made up my mind to question this, someone else brought up the question, "What about those who go to church on Sunday?" The major hesitated for a minute or so and then said, "Those who can't work on Sunday don't need to show up on Monday." A couple of Sunday's later I went to preach at several churches but came straight to work after services and nothing was said.

* * *

Harry King and I were great friends. We ran around together quite a bit. On one occasion that is hard to forget we encountered a strange thing. We had gone to a school building where a black magician named Blackburn was putting on a show. We had it in our minds that we would trick him and expose him in front of the gathering because we did not believe in that kind of stuff. We purchased our tickets at the door and walked in to take our seats. The program was already going on as we walked down the aisle. Blackburn called to us saying, "Those two men who just came in—come up here." We walked up to him and he gave us our money back and asked us to leave by the back door. Now I'm telling you, this startled us! Harry was ready to go right then, but I had other plans. Harry jumped in our car but I didn't. I waited by Blackburn's truck. We waited around outside until the show was over. Blackburn came out the back and up to his truck. He saw me standing there and I immediately challenged him. I asked him to tell my fortune. He first refused to do it. Then he took my right hand and looked at it.

He said, "You will be married before a year is up."

I told him, "I know that! I am already engaged."

"The woman you are going to marry, you don't even know now, but you will be married three times!" he replied. He added, "And you will be a wealthy man." At this remark, I went back to Harry's car and we left. This really shocked us, Harry was through with it before but now I was too! I never mentioned this to anyone again until years after I married the first time. Since then you see, I have thought about it more and more.

I continued to work for Armour for two or three Sundays straight until I received a letter stating, **"You have been chosen."**

CHAPTER 10

"You have been chosen"

*

THE NEXT THING I knew, I received a letter from "your uncle," you know, Uncle Sam, indicating that I had been drafted. It was in November and the letter stated I had a couple weeks before reporting to duty. I would have to go from Loudoun County but went back to Hume to see my mother.

The draftees met in Leesburg, Virginia by 9 AM one day in early December 1942 to board chartered buses going to Charlottesville, Virginia. A whole bunch of us were recruited at that time. Leesburg is the county seat of Loudon County. When we arrived in Charlottesville, we were inducted into the army, put on buses, "moved out smartly", and then were sent that night to Fort Meade, Maryland. At Fort Meade the following night some of us were put on guard duty and I was one. None of us had any articles read to us nor did we know military procedures. While on guard duty an officer came by and spoke to me and I spoke back. He went on about his business and came back by to me. I spoke to him again and went on my business. Then he stopped and called me to him.

He asked me, "What Company are you with?"

I responded, "Company C."

He asked, "How long have you been in the service?"

I replied, "Two days."

The next day I found out that my company commander and all his cabinet got laid out because they put a man on guard duty without knowing the articles of war.

After about a week at Fort Meade about sixteen hundred soldiers were put on a troop train and sent to the Air Navigation School in San Marcos, Texas. San Marcos was the place chosen to build a new base for the Army Air Force. They taught navigation, piloting, mechanics, and gunners to name some of the classes. I went to tail gunner school because I had come out of training as a marksman. The military staff/officers and teachers over us were brought in from Kelly Airfield in San Antonio and Randolph Field. The Hospital on the base was under the umbrella of the Brooks Army Medical Center through its opening. Kelly Field furnished the officers. A big surprise for the sixteen hundred of us black soldiers was there were no barracks for us although the white barracks were there. The army was segregated and the white barracks built first. They were in the process of building the barracks for the black soldiers but for three days we all slept on the troop train. The army brought in truckloads of tents and set them up for black soldiers while the housing was under construction. As the buildings were completed we moved into them according to units.

Here we had to complete six to eight weeks of basic training before we would be issued a pass to leave the base. My first training as a gunner ended with my first flight. When we returned to the ground I blacked out. Because of my preaching status I was put in the chaplain's corps. They had no chaplain for the black soldiers. There was no laundry facility on the base for the black soldiers' clothes. They had a laundry for the white soldiers but you couldn't mix the white's clothes with the blacks' clothes. The army had made some laundry arrangements with a black woman named Peterson in Reedville, very near the base (outside the back gate). I was selected to take the dirty clothes to her and pick up the washed clothes and return them to the soldiers. I was the only black soldier who could leave the base during that eight-week training period.

The barracks had single thickness walls; you could see the studs in the buildings. These were built to last about five years, but some of them were used for more than 27 years. The buildings were lined up on each side of the streets with the latrines in the middle of the housing quarters. The black and white soldiers didn't mix in the living quarters. The guardhouse and the motor pool were in the black section of the camp. However, we had no dealings with the whites socially, not even in the guardhouse. They had a guardhouse for both. White teachers taught the black soldiers, but in separate classrooms. Black soldiers learned how to wash airplanes, clean planes, how to do mechanic work on planes, and so forth. It didn't take much to wash you out of a position if you were black. After about a year, a lot of those black soldiers got to fly the planes, become navigators and were shipped off to officers' school. Most of the white soldiers were trained to be pilots, gunners, or navigators from the get go! After the blacks completed their training at Officer's Candidate

School, they returned to San Marcos Navigation School, but they didn't stay long. They would pick up their wings and leave. Most of them came out as warrant officers, a little lower than a second lieutenant. After the war ended, the warrant officer rank was eliminated for a while.

* * *

A typical day for me began at the Chaplain corps. I would clean up the white Chaplains desk/office and surrounding area. I never had to cut grass or do any outside work other than litter detail. It was the Chaplain that would deliver messages to the black soldiers through me. Some others would wash trucks or airplanes; some soldiers were assigned to clean the officers' barracks; they shined the officers' shoes and so on. As a private, I was making $21 a month. Later, I earned $57 a month, but I didn't have to buy my food or pay for housing. Things were pretty cheap in the forties, so I got along nicely on that monthly salary. Because I was supporting my mother when I was drafted, I set up an allotment for her for $50 dollars a month, which was the maximum I could do. That allotment lasted until my first child was born . . . but I am getting ahead of myself here!

* * *

While stationed at this base, I played a little baseball. We had a white team and a black team at the San Marcos Air Force Base. Because of the segregation laws, the white team and the black team could not play against each other. We played the teams in the town and surrounding areas. I played right field with the Air Force Team. I have always enjoyed athletics.

I quickly made the rank of private first-class. As fast as soldiers came in to the base, other soldiers were being shipped off to war. As the groups were assembled to ship out, the Chaplain would give them a talk and have prayer with them. Until he did this, I would be the one who preached and taught and counseled and prayed with them. On one occasion the Chaplain, who was white and a major, made a statement to these outgoing soldiers headed to war . . . "I will not swear to you that there is a God, because I have not seen Him." This upset me so much that I stood to my feet and in front of the troops I talked back to the chaplain. Soldiers on their way to combat didn't need to hear that kind of talk. I had to let the men in the room know that God is real. I was called in for insubordination before the Provost Marshal who was also a major. This major would not court marshal me but he blackballed me and I was never promoted. They told me if I stayed in the service for thirty years, I would still be a PFC, regardless of how well I performed. Captain Ben Hoffman had been the first chaplain and the one I trained under . . . he was a wonderful man but went off to war. The new chaplain was Major Dunn and he wasn't there long after that altercation with me. He had been on the job only a few weeks before this incident happened. If I had used a little more tact, waited until he got back to his office, and then talked about it, maybe the outcome would have been different.

* * *

I remained in the chaplain's corps for most of my time in the service, coordinating religious services for the black soldiers. I had a good deal of authority and influence on the base and in the San Marcos community because of my affiliation with the Chaplain Corp. I could go to the guardhouse and get soldiers out. For example, Pvt. John Motley was a good singer with a great bass voice. But this poor boy couldn't stay out of trouble. He was a member of a quartet we had organized on the base. When I would preach in San Marcos, Lockhart, Luling, Seguin and other surrounding areas, I would carry the base quartet with me to provide the music. I was used to carrying the Rector Sisters with me in Virginia so I kept it up in TX. Frequently, I would have to go to the guardhouse and get Motley so he could sing with the group. I could also go to the motor pool and get a bus and a driver to pick up members of local churches and bring them back to the base for services. The two chapels were on the base, a Protestant chapel and a Catholic chapel, to be used for services but we never held services in the Catholic chapel. The Jews held their services in the Protestant Chapel, also. Later, a chapel was established for the black soldiers in an empty barracks that was in the black area of the base.

Once we completed our training we were able to get passes to attend churches in town. I among others attended the First Baptist church for the first time on the second Sunday in February 1943. I immediately joined this church. The pastor of this church was Rev. Meadows and he established a rule concerning service men visiting his church. He said, "Our church lets out too late for these service men to get meals at their base so I want someone in the congregation to carry a soldier home for dinner. No one will be left out." A young lady by the name of Rosa Mae Johns selected me. (Pictured on the right).

Rev. Meadows lived quite a ways from the church; he came up on weekends to stay because his wife refused to move into the church parsonage. Not long after I joined the church, Rev. Meadows turned in his resignation. He lived in Beeville TX. Before the time he arranged to leave, his wife changed her mind and agreed to move. He came back to the church and told this to the church. The deacons of the church would not accept her change of mind and asked him to vacate his position immediately, which he did. The church immediately hired Rev. F. P. Robinson from Beaumont TX. Rev. Robinson remained pastor for several years.

* * *

At that time, Dixie Clark and I were engaged; she was a woman I met in Virginia before I came to San Marcos. When I went home on a furlough in July 1943, I discovered that my fiancé had found somebody else she wanted to be with. She didn't meet me when I came home. So, I went to her house and her mother told me she was at a dance. I went to the dance looking for her, and found her drunk. I carried her home, but I left Round Hill, Virginia that night; I decided not to continue in that relationship. I was a preacher then, and I had never seen her drunk before. I did not want to marry a woman with a drinking problem, but we still remained friends. I went back to San Marcos before my leave was up.

The congregation at First Baptist continued to take soldiers home and I continued to go home with Rosa Mae Johns. On my first visit after my furlough I asked her to marry me. Rosa Mae wanted time to think about this. It was about August 1943. She eventually agreed to marry me on the 22nd of September 1943. This was the first of Blackburn's predictions that came true. Somehow I got the notion that I had not seen her angry and wanted to see how she would react to something of which I thought she would not approve. I rented a horse and buggy and drove it down into the colored section and picked up every girl I could find. Once my wagon was loaded with all these girls I drove it uptown and right passed where she worked at the Ration Board. Now this place where she worked had huge glass windows in the front so I knew there was no doubt she would see me. I turned that buggy around and drove past the Ration Board again to carry all those girls back to where I had picked them up. I turned in the horse and buggy; walked back uptown to the Ration Board to walk Rosa Mae home when she got off work. Well, going home everything was real sweet until we got to her house. I thought then I had bitten off more than I could handle. She let me know in no uncertain terms that she did not appreciate that since we were engaged and that was not going to happen again. It took a while for this situation to quiet down but it did. Now you know, I wasn't going there anymore!

Rosa Mae's father was named Sergeant Johns. She hadn't seen him since she was three years old. Her half-sister, Clay Eula, was living in Corpus Christi when I came to San Marcos. My wife was the type of woman who meant what she said.

We were engaged to marry and went shopping at the local Piggly Wiggly grocery store. The owner, Norman Jackson mentioned to Rosa Mae something regarding our upcoming marriage. He remarked, "Rosa, I'm glad to hear that you are getting married but why do you have to marry a damn Yankee?" she just smiled and finished her shopping and left.

* * *

When Rosa Mae and I got ready to marry, Rev. Meadows couldn't be found. He was in Beeville most of the time due to his wife's refusal to move to San Marcos. Now I had the license and I wanted to get married. I found Rev. B. J. Franks who was pastor of 2nd Baptist Church (now called Greater Bethel Baptist Church). He was a great friend of my wife's people. He lived in a house he rented from her Aunt Mag's sister, Rachel. This house no longer stands but Mrs. Claude Agnes Russ lives on the lot now. Rev. Franks drove over to Rosa Mae's house to marry us on September 22nd. Attending our wedding was a girl next door named Jettie V. Norwood who heard about the wedding and came to witness it. News got out. We lived in that house with her relatives for 12 years until we could afford our own place.

Shortly after we married, an incident occurred that illustrates this aspect of her personality. I was a soldier at the time, and my wife's first cousin, John Tolliver Broadnax, had just married also. He lived in San Antonio. John had been in the army, and he was just getting home. The two new wives made plans for the both couples to meet at the theater in San Marcos so we could get acquainted. I didn't have a car then, so Rosa and I walked to the theater to meet John and his wife. We got there first so while we were waiting for John and his wife to arrive, I went to get some popcorn at a store a few doors up from the theater; my wife got in the line to get our theater tickets. When I got back to the theater, I saw my wife standing up against the wall, out of the line and noticed that she had tears in her eyes. I knew something was wrong. I walked over to her and asked what happened, what was going on . . . She pointed to a white man who was standing in the door of the theater and said "He . . ." That's all I heard her say because I turned on my heel and walked over to the man. He was the manager of the theater. Mr. Zimmerman owned the theater. Frank Funk was the manager. I asked him what he had done to my wife. He began to make a lot of gestures with his hands, and before I knew it, I had grabbed him and snatched him to me right quick. A fight started, the line broke up and to this day, I don't know what he said to hurt her feelings. Rosa rushed over to us to try to break up the fight. By that time the few people who were already inside the theater saw the fight, and they started to leave the theater. Next thing I knew, the theater was empty. In those days the white people sat downstairs, and the black people went upstairs in the balcony. When the white people started exiting, the black people began to leave also. It wasn't long before the entire theater was empty. Strangely enough, years after the fight at the theater, that man (Mr. Frank Funk) and I became real close friends.

My wife then got scared because John was coming, and she knew there could be more trouble. John was a big man, 6'5" tall and weighed about 300 lbs. He was known for his short temper, too. Rosa insisted we get away from the theatre before John arrived. In fact, when he showed up, the theater was closed because of the fight.

On our way home, my wife said, "I'll never go to the theater with you again." For forty-three years, she kept her vow. But she was like that. If she made up her mind to do something, that was it! My daughter, Mabeleen, takes after her mother. If Mabeleen tells you she's going to slap you, you better move!

CHAPTER 11

"Church business was very different then!"

*

U NDER REV. F. P. Robinson I became very active in the church. The Youth Department was my assignment and I took this very seriously; my wife was a great help to me in this even though I was still in the military.

When I left San Marcos Navigation School, I was sent to MacDill Field in Florida. Soon after my arrival at MacDill Field, I was told that my records had been lost; consequently, I couldn't get any pay for about a month and a half. My brother, James Burrell, sent me some money to help me survive until the records were located. While I was at MacDill, I taught brake repair theory. The soldiers would follow the theoretical study of brake repair with practical, hands-on work in the repair shop. While I was at MacDill, I also became an excellent marksman with a carbine rifle. From MacDill Field, I was sent to Jamaica where I was stationed when I was notified of my stepfather's death in 1944. The Army Air Force sent a plane to fly me back to Florida. I took a train from Florida to Washington, D.C. because the weather was too bad to fly. After the funeral, I didn't get a chance to go to the house with family members; I had to return immediately to Florida and on to my duty station in Jamaica.

* * *

Returning to San Marcos after being discharged, there was rumor going around town that I had left my wife and was married and living in VA. They were saying that I was already married in VA and came to TX married Rosa Mae, had two children and then returned to Virginia, can you believe that? This caused many struggles between my wife and I. While I was in Jamaica it was a secret mission and Rosa Mae didn't know where I was. No one did until I came home. By then the rumor was running rampant!

As a result of that rumor, Rosa Mae and I were having a difficult time. My wife and I had decided before we married that our children would grow up with both father and mother. As long as the Lord allowed us; both Rosa Mae and I grew up without a father and vowed this would not happen to our children. So, we remained together even though we were not intimate for four years. Rosa Mae wanted me to go out and tackle people about that rumor. But I had heard my Grandmother Molly Gaddis Washington tell somebody when I was a child, "The more you stir up shit, the more it stinks!" She would say, "You can work around a cow pie in the field all day, but if you break that crust, you are going to smell something!" That saying stuck with me. So, I wouldn't go and stir up the rumor.

Less than a day after returning to San Marcos with my discharge from the service, I stopped by Sonny Johns' gas station on Guadalupe to get my shoes shined. His son, Jackie, shined shoes in the gas station. Wallace Cheatham's father, Tommy "Blue," came in talking about the rumor. This really bothered me bad because I had just left home having had a big argument about it. Tommy Blue was talking about me while I was getting my shoes shined but he didn't know me. Sonny Johns was trying to signal Tommy to let him know that I was sitting there. I reached into my pocket and pulled out a Photostatic copy of my discharge papers. I handed the discharge paper to Tommy and asked him to read it. He read it quietly to himself. I asked him to read it again out loud, which he did.

I asked him, "When does the paper say I got out of the army?" He read the date.

I asked him, "What does the paper say?"

He said, "The paper says you got out yesterday."

I said, "Well that's when I got out of the army.

The next time you hear that lie, you straighten it out."

From that day on it was settled, that lie died almost immediately because Tommy told everyone he talked to; he was so embarrassed.

Unfortunately that didn't satisfy my wife. She felt that I should have confronted the people responsible for starting that lie. I am sure she wanted me to confront them because she knew who they were. My wife's Aunt Mary Mag was the one pushing her to get me to confront the issue publicly. Considering we were living in the house with my wife's Aunt, who had a tremendous influence on my wife; Rosa Mae believed everything she said. Rosa Mae would never contradict Mary Mag. My wife's father left when she was three years old and her mother died when she was five years old. But as time passed, Rosa Mae eventually gave up her resentment about the way I handled the rumor, and we shared a loving marriage for more than 40 years. Her help with my plumbing business was priceless. She was such an asset to me I couldn't pay her what she was worth. Just talking to her on the phone was something our customers loved to do. She helped me until her health failed.

* * *

In February of 1944, Rosa Mae and I took our first trip together and went to Washington DC to visit my mother in the hospital. A very exciting moment occurred on this trip; my wife told me she was pregnant. I was looking in a magazine at the time and saw an advertisement for Maybelline cosmetics and I liked that name. I told my wife right then if we had a girl, we would name her Mabeleen. Getting off the train we took the streetcar up to Florida Avenue to visit my Cousin Mary's beauty shop. This is where my mother would be up on the second floor. It was there that I learned Mother was in the hospital. Once again we caught the streetcar then walked to Freedman's Hospital. After we entered the hospital, we found out Mother was on the second floor and went to the staircase. Dixie Clark, my former girlfriend was coming down the stairs from visiting my mother. I introduced Rosa to Dixie and left them standing on the stairs talking. Dr. Goldenburg told my sister and others it was not doing my mother any good for her to remain in the hospital. He had the nurses teach my sister Molly how to give her injections for her pain and generally care for her then they brought her home. Rosa and Dixie became good friends and corresponded with each other for many years. Dixie was there because she and my mother were very close. Dixie knew that I was married because I had sent an invitation to the wedding. Now that may seem queer to you but I have had a lot of queer things happen all throughout my life.

* * *

Mabeleen was born August 18, 1944. My second child, Samuel Lee was born September 23, 1945. Shortly after Sammy Lee turned two years old, I received a letter from my sister in law, Pearl Burrell telling me that my mother was sick again. This time I went to see her by myself. I ended up staying from January 19th-March 3th 1947 due to a heavy snowstorm in the whole area. I went to Happy Creek VA, my sister, Molly Jackson's house; she and her husband Thor were taking care of mother. Roads were impassable. On the 3rd day of March they broke the roads through from Happy Creek to Front Royal VA. My mother told me to get my suitcase and go home. She said, "It is time for you to get back to your family in Texas." I walked behind the snow-scraper from Happy Creek to Front Royal VA where I caught the bus to Washington DC. At Union Station I caught the train to Texas.

That trip took about 28 hours before I arrived at my home in San Marcos. I arrived at 1 PM and at 3 I received a telegram from my brother in law saying my mother had passed on March 5th 1947. I have always believed that she knew how close she was and didn't want me to be there. My brother William was just 12 years old when she died. Molly took him in and raised him until he started high school. The family always took care of each other.

The very next day after I got home, the Deacons came to me asking me to preach at First Baptist. There had been a ruckus started at the church with the pastor Rev. F. P. Robinson. The deacons had found out that Rev. Robinson had bought the church building from one of the deacons, Deacon Richmond Barnett for $10 dollars. He had it recorded at the courthouse, since the church was in his name when they tried to dismiss him, he wouldn't go. When I got up to preach that Sunday, Rev. Robinson came in late and walked up to the pulpit and pushed me away. He said, "I am going to read off names of people who will no longer be members of the church." He called off 52 names and my wife and her aunt were two of them. There were no deacons in the church, even though they had come to me to ask me to be there to preach. As a matter of fact, there were no men in the church at all except me. As he read off the names the people got up and left the church. Others left the church as well. The church broke up right then.

My wife and I went home and sat down to eat dinner. While we were eating a car pulled up in front of the house. Three of the deacons had come to me to go with them to talk with the pastor. Of course I was willing to go because I really knew nothing about what was going on. When we got to the parsonage they called the pastor out to the car. He came out and walked up to the car and he said, "I will not talk to you. You will have to talk to my attorney." At that moment as I was sitting next to Deacon George Kerr I felt him move and could see he was bringing a shiny 38 special out of its holster. I grabbed his hand and held it down. The pastor saw me wrestling with Kerr so he turned and went back into the parsonage. I learned later that Deacon Lester Traywick also had his gun in the car. Deacon Willie Freeman was controlling him in the front seat while I was controlling Kerr. This mess ended up in the Supreme Court in a lawsuit. It cost the First Baptist Church $28,000. The final word from the high court said that the church was sovereign in its own and the case would have to be settled in the church. The lawyers for the church had the church pick whoever they wanted to take the case. They chose Rev. Chunn, a white Baptist church pastor. Rev. Chunn came on a specific date to meet with the church and listen to the case. They settled the case. The pastor's name was removed from the records of the courthouse and ownership of the church. It was given to new trustees. This whole case lasted about one full year. I had never in my life saw or heard of anything like this. Now I had experienced it first hand and had enough. I stayed though, and acted as the administrator, a voice of the church for about a year.

* * *

One of my favorite community-oriented groups was the Carver American Legion Post 144A. I became involved with them after I was discharged. You couldn't get in it until after you were out. It was organized in the fall of 1946, and named for Early Carver, the first Black soldier from San Marcos killed in World War II. Carver was related to the family of Ulysses Cephas, and Charter members included Sammie Hardeman, Lloyd White, Alvin Major, Charlie Williams, and Alvin Norwood. We had a gang of members, but these are all I can remember now. The white post was number 144. In Texas, black posts were always designated with the letter "A" after the number to distinguish them from the white posts. The local white American Legion set up our organization. I was the chaplain when we received our charter. We went to the army surplus store and bought guns and flags and all the materials we needed to set up a post. We turned our guns and banner over to the white post when we integrated. The white post didn't have any guns. Our flags were donated to First Baptist Church (NBC). The white post had to send out of town to get a chaplain to conduct funerals for its members, but I conducted military funerals for the black post. I was the only minister in this area who could do this for the veterans. The Tolliver-Cephas marching band would play for us when we had parades. The Smith brothers were in the band (Delores Crittenden's father and uncle; they were twins). We had a very active post, and we were very visible in the community of San Marcos.

We—the veterans had a meeting at the Dunbar School for the Colored and the Mayor Norman Jackson attended. One member, Vandora Herring spoke about how the Dunbar school had no indoor plumbing. Mayor Jackson said that it was impossible to run water uphill; the sewer line was uphill from the school. I spoke up and said, "The school could run the plumbing downhill to where there was a lift station and could be pumped back uphill to the sewer line." Mayor Jackson did not agree. He just didn't want to hear about installing a lift station or putting in plumbing for a black school. Two years later when he was no longer mayor, Jack Woods succeeded him as Mayor. At the first meeting Mayor Woods was able to put plumbing in the school. He did whatever it took to do this! There was no plumbing on Centre Street at that time. The City installed sewer lines from Endicott Street where the school was located down to Charlie Williams' house at the end of Centre Street. The school didn't have any trouble with the sewerage because it didn't go up Comal Street to a lift station; I told Mayor Jackson the sewerage would work fine if they ran the line down to the lift station that was located next to Marvin Merriweather's house on MLK. The veterans stayed on this until it was completed. Mayor Woods got the job done; not only for the school but for many streets in that area. He worked hard for the colored people. He was able to receive a grant to do the work.

CHAPTER 12

"Education is Important"

*

THE GUADALUPE BAPTIST Association, of which the First Baptist church was a member, sent Rev. M. C. Arnold to the church in 1948. They sent him as soon as they heard the church lawsuit had been settled. He was immediately accepted as the new pastor. Rev. Charles Connelly, one of the officers of the Association and former pastor of First Baptist (from 1927 to 1938) lived in Kyle, only seven miles from the church. He had a great interest in the church. His advanced age prohibited him from driving his car as frequently as he had; so he asked me to drive him wherever he needed to go. Sometimes he would drive from Kyle to San Marcos and then turn the wheel over to me. He told Rev. Arnold I was too good a person to be wasted and asked the Reverend, as pastor, to get the church to pay my way through Guadalupe College. The Guadalupe College was under the umbrella of The Guadalupe Baptist Association. I will always be grateful to Rev. Connelly, for making it possible for me to study at Guadalupe College in the 1950s. I didn't pay one penny for my education at Guadalupe College. Guadalupe College gave me a sound educational foundation that helped me to succeed in my ministry and in my business. Rev. Grant would drive us (Reverends Arnold, James, and Washington) to Seguin. Rev. Hall is the only person I know who remembers my days at Guadalupe College because we were classmates.

We had some outstanding teachers at the College a seminary that taught New Testament and Old Testament, Greek, Hebrew, English, math, biblical history, homiletics, etc. Dr. Merriweather taught church doctrine. Dr. Murray taught church history. Dr. Johnson, the president of the college, taught Greek. He could teach anything in the curriculum. C.C. Brown, the vice-president of the college, could teach a variety of courses. Dr. Johnson was a brilliant teacher. He could take any word and recite its origin. He never had to use a book. Dr. Martin believed the teacher was responsible for enabling the student to learn. He often said, "If the student hasn't learned, the teacher hasn't taught." Dr. Martin told us that we didn't have to memorize everything, but we should know where to find information when we needed it. Dr. Johnson had memorized a vast body of knowledge. He never used notes in his lectures. Even when he was preaching, Dr. Johnson didn't use notes or an outline. He would read the scripture on which his sermon was based; then he would lay down that Bible and preach. He reminds me of my current pastor at Mount Morris Baptist Church in Hume Virginia, Rev. Dr. Lindsay O. Green.

Guadalupe College was a wonderful place to study. Most of my classes met in the mornings. I knew Students from Bastrop, Gonzales, Austin, etc. Josie Meyers was an outstanding student from San Marcos. In addition to classrooms and dormitories, we had a library and a dining room. My friend, Rev. Hall (who later became moderator of the Guadalupe District Association) and his sister were my classmates. At certain times during the semester, we had to preach before our classmates. They would critique our sermons and give us suggestions on how we could improve. At this point Rev. Arnold licensed me in the First Baptist Church. The First Baptist Church maintained a close fellowship with all other churches and denominations. I was also involved with a group of ministers (Rev. C. L. Luddington and others) who organized the Christian Fellowship Union. The white and black people in San Marcos got to know me first as a result of my work in the chaplain's corps.

I remember one occasion when I had driven Rev. Connelly to a meeting at the college, and he discovered that the college owed a passed due debt that needed to be paid. Rev. Connelly said, "Take me back home." He went out to his field and caught a cow, put a rope on it and led the cow to Kyle and sold it. I drove him back to the college, and he turned the money over to the board to pay the outstanding debt.

* * *

It was 1947 and I was working for a plumber, S. H. Shaffer. In 1947 the state of Texas came out with a law that all plumbers needed to have a license to do plumbing. We had to apply for the license. I was given a journeyman license in '47. The work I did far exceeded the license I had. I was estimating his work and keeping his books when he was not there. I was making $.75 hour for a 40-hour week. In the mid 50's Shaffer took a trip to a new business he was opening in Fort Worth TX, over a hundred miles away. He left me in charge. A person came in to pay his bill, which I could not find. I called Shaffer and asked his wife where the bill was. She told me and when I got the bill, it was incomplete. I subsequently found out that he was charging $5 per hour and paying me .75 cents. This urged me to start my own business and have my wife help me.

At this same time San Marcos had opened a veteran's trade school, Hays County Vocational School for electricians, plumbers, refrigeration and auto mechanics. The superintendent of the school was Jack Sledge. I enrolled in that school to take plumbing. There ended up being no teacher for the plumbing class so I took auto mechanics. Later when they hired a plumbing teacher I transferred to that class and graduated. I'm telling you that education is important, but the help of the Lord is more important! Because they felt I held the church together during the lawsuit, the Lord saw fit to educate me through the church.

CHAPTER 13

"The Whites Began to Help Me"

*

MAYBE THESE SEEM to be strange bedfellows but my church work and my plumbing business assisted each other. Recall now that Rev. Arnold our new pastor has come on the scene during a very traumatic period in the life of the First Baptist Church. He was thrust in the middle of a church with no organization and had to immediately begin to make order out of chaos. Members had scattered like wild goats under the attack of wolves. There was a lack of love in the membership; backbiting, lying, families rising up against each other. The family of the deacon that sold the church was still in the church. It was hard let me tell you . . . and I was the person who had to deal with this mess for three years while the church was in court. The Lord blessed me though; I came through it. This is why Rev. Arnold used me as he did. He gave me the Youth and the Junior & Senior Missionary Departments. These were the groups that stayed together. From an early age I had developed a love of children and they became my primary concern now. During this time I had begun to write the programs for Vacation Bible School and other Youth Department activities. This was before the days of computers . . . it was all done by hand.

During these four years, three of the lawsuit and first year that Rev. Arnold came, I began working part-time at Shaffer's and spent the four years in school supporting my family with this and part-time work for myself, outside of Shaffer's business.

Rev. Arnold could see that the church was in dire need of fixing up. The front steps leading up into the church were nothing but rotten wood (nine feet of steps to the front door), the roof leaked and the heating and cooling system was useless. He had to get the church together first. He couldn't start working on the building or other repairs on the church until they came together. He obtained the Smith Bros. Contracting Co. They were the biggest company in the black community and they were twins. The plumbing was terrible in the church; I took on the plumbing myself but I had no license. The wiring, plumbing and many other things I did without my license. This is where the white people in San Marcos began to rally around me. It was under the umbrella of the local white people in the community who helped me during the four years of pure struggle and now that Rev. Arnold was trying to get things rolling with the church, they came to me and let me know that I could depend on them. However, I only used them in a pinch situation. I want to give credit to two old white master plumbers who got licensed back in 1947. Because of their age they only took small jobs. Occasionally they deliberately took larger jobs and gave the work to me, getting my permits to do the work. These kept the law off me most of time. I was able to work from 1948 until 1962 plumbing with the white master plumbers. They were such a help to me at a time when segregation was running rampant. Credit goes to Earl Koons and Roger Herd.

Shortly after this, I encountered a situation that set me back a bit financially and in my business. It caused me to lose faith a little bit at first. I had purchased an old car that had a rumble seat in it. I used this rumble seat like you would a truck. On my way up Austin Street, the main street through the college area, one of the college trucks came out of a side road and broadsided me on the passenger side. When this accident happened it caused my tools and toolbox to fly out of the rumble seat scattering them out over the street. One of the college policemen came on the scene wanting to talk to me about what happened. I was in the process of retrieving my tools from the street and this aggravated him to the point that he backed me up against a rock wall with a billy club up in my face. I asked him to let me get my tools because other people began help themselves to them. He just threatened me by begging me to move so that he could bust my head open. It took a great deal of restraint on my part to remain still while my tools were being stolen in front of my eyes. This 'officer' allowed this to happen, just further underscoring my distrust of the law and their desire to protect me, a black man.

After this I tried to get a lawyer to help me because the car was so damaged that it could not be fixed. Every lawyer I went to asked me the same question, "What did you pay for the car?" I bought it privately for $60 and no lawyer would take the case. Of course the car was worth much more than this. Their answer to me was that the college had lawyers and it would not be worth it to them to fight the college lawyers over a $60 car.

* * *

There was an incident when I had contracted a new plumbing job (which included a car from Mrs. Miller); one of the white plumbers saw me working this job and reported me to the inspectors and police. They came out and arrested me, taking me before Judge Callahan at the courthouse. While the case was going on Earl Koons heard about it and came into the courthouse. He walked right into Judge Callahan's courtroom. He saw me standing there being questioned.

He interrupted the whole court proceedings by hollering out loud, "Boy, what are you doing here? My work is going undone and you're standing up here arguing with these folks!"

The Judge said, "Oh Earl, is this your job he's been working on?"

Earl replied, "Yes, and the statute of limitations is running out on it!"

The Judge shouted, "Case dismissed!" I went on out and back to work; from then on they were very careful what they did to me! At least until this happened.

While working on the church, an old white licensed electrician named Smith was the one who obtained the permits for me to do the electric work. Roger Herd, the plumber obtained the permits for me to do the plumbing on the church. Without the help of these two white men we would have been in bad shape trying to get the church in good working order. The work on the church was finished in 1952.

* * *

Back in 1946 I became a Master Mason in the Silver Leaf Lodge Number 215. As you might expect the white lodges and blacks were separate. On a trip to Kerrville (about 105 miles from San Marcos) in the early 1950s I had an experience involving a white mason that I had never seen before. Rev. Arnold and about five other cars were en route to an afternoon service at the Mt. Olive Baptist Church where Rev. Everidge was the pastor. We were all following Rev. Arnold. I was the last car and carrying my family with me. We came to a town, Burnie TX about 15 miles before you get to Kerrville, when suddenly a car following me, passed me on the left and crossed in front of my car to make a right turn into a gate off the road. I hit the other driver's taillight and knocked it out. The steering column on my car was disabled in the wreck, so I couldn't steer or stop the car and it ran into an embankment. It was completely out of the lanes of traffic. In the crash the back seat of the car flew out through the doors. We could not account for the baby, Willie. The impact of the wreck knocked Willie out of the car. It took us quite a while to find him after the accident. I saw the backseat of the car and went to pick it up and put it back in the car. It had been thrown into a ditch, and the back seat had landed over Willie. A woman who had just driven up came over and took my wife and the children to the Kerrville hospital. He suffered a dislocated collarbone in the wreck. No one else was hurt.

The police were called to investigate the accident and the highway patrol showed up. By this time, my wife and children had been taken to the hospital. A crowd of white people had gathered around the wreck. Because the back wheels of my car were sitting on the edge of the hard surface part of the road, the policeman ordered me to move my car. I tried to tell him the steering was broken and I could not move it. I had already tried to move it. I had already talked to a wrecker to move it but he wanted $35, which I didn't have! Now the policeman wants me to get it moved. He began to swing his club around my body and head in a very threatening manner. I began to give the Masonic distress signal since I was a Mason. I would give the signal and look over the crowd for a response, but nobody responded. The policeman was following me so I kept someone between him and me to keep him from hitting me. Then I started to give the Masonic distress signal again, and I saw a white man on the other side of the crowd who was answering my signal. I immediately moved through the crowd till I was next to him. When the policeman kept insisting that I move my car, the white Mason intervened and told the policeman, "I'll move it when I get ready. That car is under my control, I am taking over that car now." The policeman couldn't harass me anymore after the white Mason spoke up on my behalf. Rev. Everidge soon arrived at the scene of the accident, he came straight to me and took me to the car; he carried me to Kerrville for the church service. I sure felt a lot better when I saw Rev. Everidge drive up.

Not only did the white mason answer my distress call, but also he insisted on getting my car repaired for me. He asked for my name and telephone number and indicated that he would call me when my car was ready. A couple of days later, he called and Rev. Arnold took me to pick up my car. I had to appear before the magistrate before I could get it. It cost me $9 to get the car and the hospital bill was $5 for bandages. I'll never forget that Mason who came to my rescue when I really needed a friend. I only wish I knew his name. One name I know who helped me that day was Jesus.

CHAPTER 14

"The Sixties Were Even Better Years"

*

A NUMBER OF both white and black Baptist Churches were without pastors in 1956. Rev. M. C. Arnold took me, in the middle of a week to a black church in Lockhart TX by the name of Mason Lone Oak Baptist. A Rev. Mason organized Mason Lone Oak Baptist Church in 1866 or 1867. Because the first church building was located near a solitary oak tree, it became known as Mason Lone Oak Baptist Church. They needed a pastor. Thirteen pastors had served the congregation in the previous twenty-one years. Two of those pastors stayed nine years. Rev. McClure stayed six years and Rev. Ray stayed three years. These men preceded me. They stayed longer than any of the other pastors. Rev. McClure went to Kansas to pastor after he left Mason Lone Oak. Rev. Ray just walked out, leaving the church in a mess. This is where I come in to the picture.

The 2nd Sunday in February, I preached my first sermon at that church. The deacons became quite moved by my sermon and asked me to come back on the 4th Sunday; they had services 2 Sunday's a month. After the service on the fourth Sunday the church called me to be their pastor. I did not accept at that time, but told them I would be back on the next 2nd Sunday in March to preach. I committed to continue to preach for them through April when I accepted the call to pastor there. My pastorate began on the 2nd Sunday in May 1956. This was my first church pastorate. The church was located six miles outside of the town. When the church was originally built there, many families were all around. Time and death changed all that. As the older people died, the young ones sold the land and moved on. Only one family remained near the church, the George Ellison's, who lived a half mile from it. There was another family who had a farm about five miles from the church by the name of Lawyer Adair; his brother Cass lived in town. Cass's wife was the secretary at the church.

As I began my pastorate at Mason Lone Oak, the church was trying to get rid of Deacon George Ellison. I don't know the whole story, but I found out that the previous pastor, Pastor Ray and Deacon George Ellison went to a bank in Lockhart and borrowed money to buy forty-five or fifty hogs. I don't know Rev. Ray's side of the story. But Deacon Ellison claimed that most all the hogs got cholera and the government killed them, preventing them from selling the hogs to raise enough money to pay off the bank loan. The church had stood for the loan. The default on the loan left the church in a bad spot. The deacons were getting ready to put George Ellison off the deacon board. Since Rev. Ray just up and walked out on the church that put George responsible to the church for the debt. I knew that all of this was coming up in my first business meeting at the church; it was set for Saturday morning at 9 o'clock. I took out a loan in San Marcos on Friday evening, and I took the money to George Ellison's house.

I told George, "After devotions in the morning, I want you to turn this money in to the church as the first order of business." My idea was to kill anything foul before it got started. At the meeting, George put the money on the table and said, "This is the money for the hogs." With that the whole hog business was settled. It was worth it to me to get the hog loan dispute cleared up so as not to have that issue creating any more conflicts in the church. Lee Brown got up and said, "Rev. Washington is here. We're tired of jumping from one preacher to another; it gives the church a bad name." Lee Brown was chairman of the Deacon Board at the time.

The secretary, TO Adair, that was her name, not two initials, gave me the church record book right after I accepted the call to pastor the church. Over the next few months I had time to read it and learned that they were supposed to have seventy-two members in the church. At this point I wanted to find those members. Frequent visits to the city of Lockhart looking for members revealed that there were only twenty-six members and nineteen of them attended the church. Many of them were dead and some had moved away. The only young people who came to church were the two Ellison children and I baptized both of them! Mabeleen and Willie were the only other children who were in this church and May played the piano for me. I had done some plumbing for a real estate man and this man had repossessed a house that had a piano in it. This man sold me the piano in exchange for the work I did for him. I carried that piano to my house and hired a lady to come to my house and teach Mabeleen how to play.

* * *

It was plain to see that I had to make a bunch of changes. The first change I made was to begin having Sunday school. Holding Sunday school only two Sunday's a month was just not going to work. We had Sunday school every Sunday, and church services every Sunday, too. At first I used my Boyd's Sunday school book from First Baptist and typed up (with my old hunt and peck system) the lesson to pass out. I made handouts at that time. When I left the Chaplains Corps, and the base closed, they were getting rid of old surplus. The Chaplain gave me an old Underwood typewriter and a mimeograph machine that I used for years. I would later replace this Underwood with a Smith Corona portable!

The Deacons Protective Association was an association made up of deacons and their wives. It was designed to protect the church from the pastor. I can't really say they were effective in this church. It was a racket you catch what I mean! The Association wanted to have its quarterly meeting at Mason Lone Oak. I didn't approve of that plan and told the deacons, "You are overloading yourself. I am a new pastor here. I think you should put off the Association meeting until I can get better acquainted with the church." They agreed not to host the Association.

Three years passed before I decided to move this church from the country into town. Even this idea to move wasn't brought up to the church until I had been there two years. The building had a square top with a peak in the middle, and all four sides were equal. There was a vision I had for the church and that was not it. I didn't like that style. When the movers came and removed the roof to move the building to the new site, I took advantage of this opportunity to redesign the roof and add a room on the back. It was 1959; it's on the cornerstone of the church.

Right up front, as pastor of Mason Lone Oak, I was told that the Adair's, a prominent family in the congregation, had been responsible for several pastors leaving the church. When the pastors in the Guadalupe Association heard that I had accepted this church, they said they would give me six months before I would be gone. The pastor/members of the local A.M.E. church and a lot of other folks in the community also predicted that I would not last longer than six months as pastor. I was the talk of the town and the surrounding area. This was due to the church's reputation for getting rid of pastors after only a short tenure and the condition of the church building. Speaking of the condition of the building, I remember standing in the pulpit and looking up at the moon through the ceiling and roof.

* * *

I knew that the Lord sent me there. Everywhere I went, I knew it was the Lord that sent me. Even the move to Texas, I knew the Lord sent me. Every move I made was to prepare me for the next. They had three or four other preachers to come preach during the time I was the interim pastor. One Saturday, after I had been there over two years, I received the first of many visions to move the church. You could say, I was playing Nehemiah who went by night to examine the walls of the city. Like Nehemiah, I quietly devised a plan for the move; I found the land and looked into the cost of moving and remodeling the building, but I waited for the right time to present this vision to the church. I found a whole new section in town to which people were building houses and moving houses. The University of Texas was buying up lots to expand the university to these towns. So, I purchased a lot for the church and decided to move the church into that area. I planned to bring up the topic of the move at a business meeting on a Saturday but nobody showed up except Lawyer Adair. He and I walked around on the church ground and talked. I shared my vision with him. He listened closely. At the next business meeting all the deacons were present.

When the meeting was almost over, I called on Deacon Adair to tell the church about something that we had discussed. He explained my plans for moving the church into town. Lee Brown then got up and said, "Lawyer Adair has been a deacon in this church for fifteen years, and that is the first topic that he has ever brought before the church. Let's vote on it before he changes his mind!" Somebody quickly seconded Lee's motion and the matter was settled. Lawyer Adair went home that day and never returned until the day of the dedication of the church in its new location. Rev. Stewart, who was Moderator of the Guadalupe District, didn't want me to move the church. In fact, nobody in the district wanted me to move Mason Lone Oak. They talked against me like nobody's business for moving that church, but, "I didn't pay that no mind because the Lord had told me to move the church." I installed the plumbing in the remodeled church and Rev. M.C. Arnold (who was then pastor of 19th Street Baptist Church in Austin) preached the dedication service. I remained pastor at Mason Lone Oak for 24 years; although there were several times I almost left.

* * *

By July of 1960, the manager at Wonder Caves Amusement Park was Mr. Frank Funk; Mr. Buddy Mostyn was the owner. Mr. Mostyn decided to refurbish the whole park including the restrooms. Also, they had discovered another chamber in the caves that Mr. Mostyn wanted to open to the public. He asked for bids from plumbers to do the plumbing. The manager, Mr. Funk, met me up town one day and said: "Washington, we are refurbishing and enlarging Wonder Caves. We have been accepting bids for the plumbing work. I want you to submit a bid." I still didn't have my license but he handed me the blueprint and told me to have a bid ready by 1:00 o'clock that afternoon. I went home and prepared my bid and jumped in my truck and drove up to the Wonder Caves office and gave it to Mr. Funk. When I walked in the office, Mr. Funk said: "Man, you just got here in time. We are opening sealed bids." Because my bid was much lower than all the others, I got the job. In order for me to get any work, I had to be cheaper than the other plumbers. But I still made a profit. Mr. Mostyn was in the pecan business, as well. He bought and sold pecans wholesale. The Wonder Caves Park was outside of the city limits in the 1950s, therefore I did not need a license to do plumbing work. This is the same man with whom I had a fight with at the theatre years before. He built a new store seven miles outside of town and called it *The Pecan Center* and sold pecans in hundred pound sacks. I plumbed that store after I finished Wonder Cave Park.

People would talk about the water that ran up hill at Wonder Caves. I installed that system when I upgraded the plumbing in the restrooms. Well, during the time I was working at the Wonder Caves, Mr. Funk and I became good friends. We never mentioned the altercation at the theater. I did all his plumbing at his home after I finished the Wonder Caves job. He lived on the corner at East Bishop and San Antonio Streets. Even after he died, I kept the plumbing up in their home for his wife. Both Mr. Mostyn and Mr. Funk became customers of mine.

* * *

It was 1962 and I had been working at the Baptist Academy since 1961. A great man I'll never forget was Jack Major. Jack knew everything I was doing. By now I had been doing plumbing since 1952. Jack was appointed the head electrical inspector in San Marcos, and he was the Fire Marshall too. Jack was a thorough man. He received numerous complaints about my working without a Master Plumber's license. The two new plumbers in town called Jack and told him they had seen that "bootlegger" plumber working. I was working on Mr. Bert Miller's house; he had the drug store in town. Rusty O'Bryant, one of them, had called Jack and told him that he had seen me working for Mr. Miller; Gene Funk, the other plumber, also complained about my doing plumbing for Mr. Miller.

The greatest year of my plumbing career came in 1962 with the opportunity to get my Master Plumber's license. The local plumbers continued to complain about my work to a man named, Mr. Lynn Brown, Chief Administrator of the State Plumbing Board in Austin. Mr. Brown came to San Marcos to investigate these complaints. He talked with Jack Major and Jack took him around town and showed him my work. Then he brought Mr. Brown up to the Baptist Academy where I was working. Jack knew that I had applied for my license twice, but the board had refused to accept my application. In May of 1962, the inspector caught me plumbing at the Academy. Lynn got tired of receiving complaints about that "one black man in San Marcos." It was about 10:00 in the morning when he arrived at the Academy. I was down on my knees, setting a commode in a restroom (on the boys' side) in the gymnasium in the basement on Academy Street. I heard footsteps coming up behind me. The floor was cement with carpet on it. I looked back in the direction of the sound, and saw a big pair of shiny cowboy boots; I looked up, and there stood Lynn Brown, over six feet tall, wearing western cut jeans and a big cowboy hat. I looked behind him and saw Jack Major, and then I knew what the visit was about. I got up to talk to the men.

I said, "I guess y'all caught me."

Mr. Brown said, "Yeah, we caught you all right." Jack didn't say anything.

Mr. Brown said, "Mr. Washington"—(now that was unusual in this area for a white person to address a black man as "Mr.")—but he said, "Mr. Washington, you know you can't do plumbing without a license." I told him that I had applied for a license twice, but my applications had been rejected. He said, "That won't happen again. You have to get a license, and you have to quit working now." I picked up my tools, and the two men left. They stopped at the office and told Mr. Floyd Patterson, the manager of the Academy, that they had caught me working without a license and that I could not work until I got one. I was walking down the hill on my way to the truck when I met Floyd.

He asked, "What would it take for you to get your license?"

I said, "Whatever it takes for me to get a hold of $132.00."

He said "Go by the office and tell the secretary to make out a check for $132.00, payable to the Texas State Plumbing Board."

I mailed the check along with the application that Mr. Brown gave me in the gymnasium. In about a week, I got a letter from the Plumbing Board, telling me when to come for my examination.

Now in those days, I didn't have dependable transportation, but the Academy loaned me a pickup truck to drive up to Austin for the test. I didn't know that there was no spare tire. It had a lug wrench, tire tool, and jack but no spare. I had a flat near Oltorf Street in Austin. There was a filling station nearby; I pulled off the road, removed the flat and rolled it down to the filling station and had it fixed. I put the tire back on and continued on my way to the Texas State Plumbing Board. I knew where it was located because I had been up there several times previously, in an attempt to take the test. You understand what I mean? When I arrived, the man administering the test said, "You are an hour late. The test started at 8:00 this morning." I told him about the flat tire that delayed me.

He said, "We'll give you another test date."

But I said, "No, I have been trying for years to get my license, and I'm here, so I'll take the test today."

He said "You're putting yourself at a disadvantage if you start an hour late." I assured him that I still wanted to take the test, and he agreed to let me get started.

The man gave me three sheets of paper and a blueprint. I had to read the blueprint to determine what plumbing needed to be installed. Then I had to fill out a sheet requesting materials to meet the specifications that were indicated in the blueprint. The installation had to be State compliant. I turned in my supply list, and he issued the materials that I requested. The materials for the test were small pieces of wood, not real plumbing materials. I could go back twice to request different materials. Each time a person requested a change in materials beyond the first two; seven points were deducted your test score. By noon, I had filled out my supply request forms, received my materials, and started installing the plumbing. We were expected to use proper nomenclature for plumbing materials and spell everything correctly. We were evaluated on our ability to read a blueprint, name and select materials, as well as the quality of our installations.

When lunchtime came, I sat down and ate my sack lunch. I went right back to work after I finished my meal. Around 3:00 in the afternoon. I had completed the test.

The test administrator asked, "Are you through?" I said yes.

And he said, "Are you sure? I want you to be sure because you don't get a second chance." I assured him that I had finished the examination. Two weeks later, I received my license; I had made 98 on the test. Now I can't hardly describe the feeling I had after struggling three years to accomplish this feat! I bought my store license and certificate to collect taxes and boy I was hooked up now! I had these all hanging on my wall.

* * *

For several years, I worked as a plumber for the San Marcos Baptist Academy, even before I received my license. Also, I was in a plumbing partnership with a white plumber named Jim Gentry. Jim decided to take a job as crew leader of plumbers at Southwest Texas State University, but in order to join the union; he had to close his plumbing business. But we already had work in progress, so he turned the business over to me, and that's how I got acquainted with the plumbing wholesale businesses. I could buy supplies wholesale, even though I didn't have a license. For example, if a commode cost $75.00, I could get it for $40.00 wholesale and sell it to the Academy for $45.00 or whatever. I never cut the price of supplies below 33 1/3 percent of the wholesale price. The Academy was able to get its plumbing done cheaper because of my association with the wholesalers during my partnership with Jim Gentry. Because I didn't have a master plumber's license, I had to work for the wages of a journeyman plumber, which resulted in another savings for the Academy.

* * *

Before I was working for the academy, I was doing work for a helicopter training facility, which later became known as the Gary Job Corps. Dick Montague, Director of Maintenance at Gary, called and asked me to come and show them the location of where there was a specific water cut off. The records indicated where the cut off should be found, but the building had been enlarged 50 feet in the years after the water cut off was installed, and Dick had forgotten this. Therefore, Mr. Montague was looking for the cut off in the wrong place. When I went out to help find it, and I reminded them that 50 feet had been added to the building. You see I had been working at Gary years before when the addition to the building had been constructed. I measured 50 feet from where Mr. Montague had been digging and said "Dig right here." Bingo! The pick hit the cut off pipe. Mr. Montague asked, "How in the world did you know where to look?" I reminded him again of the 50-foot addition, and he realized his mistake.

Dick was impressed with me and said, "I have been authorized to hire some more workers." He offered me a starting salary of $1.05 an hour more than what I was earning at the Academy. So, I gave the Academy two weeks notice and took the job at Gary. Mr. Patterson, Academy Administrator came to me while I was working on a steam heater and said, "If my enrollment wasn't off by 100 students, I would pay would you the same salary that Gary offered." But I tell you; I didn't want my salary to depend on the Academy's enrollment. If his enrollment dropped so would my salary!

* * *

I went to work at Gary as foreman over the plumbing for the entire facility. In fact, I installed the plumbing in most of the 23 new dormitory buildings at Gary, and did much of it by myself. I hired Johnnie Bratton to take care of the simple plumbing repairs, so that I could install plumbing in the new dormitories. Johnnie had been a black plumber in the army; he retired from the army as a master sergeant. He was looking for a job, and I tried to get him to go into business with me in San Marcos. But he was afraid that he couldn't handle that level of plumbing work. He was not confident that his plumbing work would pass the inspection of local inspectors. This would be the first time he encountered inspectors.

Gloria Wright Leonard, Mrs. Claude Agnes Russ' daughter, was secretary at the Southside Community Center while I served as president. Gloria would call me at Gary and remind me of meetings and other activities I was supposed to attend. I couldn't have kept up with my plumbing business, my job at Gary, and my community service work without Gloria's help. She was the best secretary I ever had in those days.

* * *

I bought a lot on Texas Avenue in February 1956 and built the house on it. They started the house in April and finished it in August. I moved into the house September 1st, 1956. Meanwhile in about 1954 that area was incorporated into the extra territory jurisdiction of the city and rezoned industrial. I was on the Planning and Zoning commission for the city at that time. Homesteads were not supposed to be built in that area. I was able to get around this by making my plumbing shop part of my home. It adjoined my home on Texas Avenue. The plumbing shop was obtained when I bought the building from Gary (a former latrine building) and connected it to my house and set up my office in there.

About seven years into my pastorate at Mason Lone Oak, I think it was around 1963; I had my first heart attack. It was the year that Sam my oldest son graduated from high school, that's how I remember, catch what I mean? I was working at the Baptist Academy, and the day before my heart attack, I was driving down the hill from the Academy on the way home from work. I noticed a man and little girl standing on the corner of Hutchison and Mary Street. He was reading something, but she was holding his hand. All of a sudden she let go and darted into the street in the path of my car just as I was crossing the street. I almost stopped when I saw them standing there to let them cross and noticed he was just reading something. I may have given her the notion that I would stop when she darted out. I hit the brakes and stopped, but she was so small a child that I couldn't see her in front of my car. When the man heard my brakes screeching, he looked up and saw the little girl in the street. He ran into the street to get her. He looked at me and said, "You didn't hit her." I think the incident scared me so much it contributed to the heart attack, which I had the next day.

Early in the morning, I called Rev. Singleton, pastor of the black First Baptist Church in San Marcos. I asked him if I could catch a ride to San Antonio where he was to speak at the Guadeloupe Association Sunday School Congress Board Meeting. Later that evening, after the morning session, I began to feel sick and decided to come back home. At lunch I had even bought a soft drink thinking I had some indigestion but that didn't help. Rev. John Bailey, pastor of St. John Baptist Church in Kenwood was leaving the meeting to go back to his church.

"Are you going by the bus station?" I asked.

He said, "I can go by there, if you wish to go."

We left together and just got to the bus station just in time. The bus was ready to pull out; I didn't even go in the station and paid my fare on the bus.

The bus route went about one hundred yards past my house. I got off the bus and walked up to my house. When I reached the top step, I fell forward on the porch. My son, Samuel, was sitting in the living room watching the TV with the front door open. Sam saw me fall and jumped up saying, "Daddy!" He rushed outside and picked me up and carried me to the car. He didn't even go back in the house but he hollered back and told his mother, "I'm taking daddy to the doctor!" I don't remember what happened in the Dr's office but I was told that Dr. Sowell said, "Carry your father into the examining room and lay him on the table. Dr. Sowell was an old man then, but he was a good doctor. The doctor said, "I have been looking for this to happen," referring to my heart attack. I was burning the candle at both ends, if you catch what I mean, ripping and running involved in so many things.

After this was part of my past, I went in to the doctor and asked him why he didn't tell me that I was at risk for a heart attack. I really blessed him out that he didn't tell me this but he just said, "Now, if I had told you, what would you have done about it?" "I don't know," I replied. There would have to be a recuperation period after this heart attack that lasted about four months. Dr. Crook, President of the Academy, called Dr.

Sowell to report my condition to him. He then called me and asked me if I felt up to supervising some plumbing work that needed to be done. My doctor allowed me to work approximately two hours each day during my recovery period. With the doctor's permission I would go up to the Academy in the mornings and supervise the plumbing work, although I was not allowed to lift anything at all.

After a short time I was strong enough to return to Mason Lone Oak on Sundays, but I didn't preach. At the church I had several Associate Ministers who did the preaching while I was recuperating. The Warren brothers, Bobby and William, were two of my associate ministers and were outstanding preachers. I pretty much left them in charge. After several months of rest, I was able to go back to work full time at the Academy and to resume my duties as pastor at the church and my other civic obligations.

* * *

You could say that I evangelized that neighborhood! I made these extra trips (in my spare time, ha!) to the community of Lockhart and did what I could to recruit a bunch of young people for the church. It was a slow but blessed progress and at one time, we had 17 military men and women in the church. Holding services every Sunday, we never had a hundred members in the 24 years that I pastored the church. Now even so, the members we did have were working members. Most of them were young people that I had baptized; I held Bible classes, choir rehearsals, and I organized the mixed church baseball team. The association really got on me for this.

Mrs. Ella Brown, mother of Lee Brown, was the head of the missionary program. Now let me tell you, she was good and she stayed with it, even when the church was without a pastor. This was mainly because she was an outstanding member; she would go to the Association every year as a self-appointed standing delegate. When Ella Brown died, I asked Mrs. Ella Mae Ellison to take her place. She accepted this and went to the Association. She came back and made her report to the church. At this time I had to work to get her to be the standing delegate, even though she was hesitant at first to take on that responsibility. The church paid her way. She did a beautiful job with the missionary program and as the standing delegate to the Association. The Association met at different churches in Texas. Our church hosted the November Board, a one-day meeting for the Association that made arrangements for all the annual work. Lockhart was noted for its barbeque sausage and people from miles around would love to come to our church because they knew we would go to Black's Barbeque for lunch on this one-day meeting. I made all those arrangements and Black's let us meet in one room and would count the plates to give us a bill, which was paid by the Association.

* * *

My love for children caused me to bring Vacation Bible School (VBS) for the youth at Mason Lone Oak, but my plumbing business and my job at the Baptist Academy did not allow time for me to run it myself. Rev. Byron and I were talking one day at the Academy. His church was a member of the Southern Baptist Convention (SBC). The SBC was the umbrella under which the Academy operated. Dr. William Crook who had worked for President Lyndon Johnson as the Ambassador to India ran the Academy. Rev. Byron was pastor of the white First Baptist Church on Hutchison Street in San Marcos where Dr. Crook was a member. I mentioned my interest to Rev. Byron in setting up a VBS in Lockhart. He actually volunteered to organize a staff from the youth of his church and send them to Mason Lone Oak to conduct the Vacation Bible School. Now this was a white church that welcomed blacks and even had a few members there. I didn't have enough people to run a bible school as most of my adult members were away picking cotton. Rev. Byron's team of young people came to Lockhart two or three summers to conduct our weeklong VBS. They brought their own teaching materials and paid their own transportation costs. The VBS didn't cost Mason Lone Oak or me a dime. I made sure that this program was available to our whole community. The good will shown by the youth of Dr. Byron's church so impressed my grandson, Sean Kevin, who attended the VBS in Lockhart, that he eventually joined First Baptist with my permission. He was one of a small number of black people who were members of that church.

* * *

It was 1964 and I served Mason Lone Oak as their pastor for eight years without a salary; I got what was left over after the bills were paid. I wasn't hurting for money because my plumbing and other work was doing great. There came a time when two deacons from the black Baptist church in Hillsboro, TX came to Mason Lone Oak for a Sunday morning service. One of these deacons was a relative of the Brown family... Deacon Lawyer Brown and he had visited the church with his people several times. He had brothers, nieces and nephews in my church. He knew what Mason Lone Oak had been and what it was now. After the service they came to my office and the other deacon said, "We have been sent by our church in Hillsboro to call you to pastor our church. We are without a pastor." Of course I needed time to think about this sudden development. I asked for thirty days to think on it and give them an answer.

Within the month timeframe I had given the deacons from Hillsboro, the members decided to sponsor a "Pastor's Anniversary" program to raise some money to show appreciation for my eight years of service at Mason Lone Oak. Deacon Adair fought against the anniversary program. When he did that, I had almost made up my mind that I was going to leave the church. I had discussed this with my wife, Rosa Mae and she advised me not to go because of my growing business in San Marcos. I was really hurt about that meeting where Deacon Adair fought against me having any salary at all. All alone on my way to church that Sunday morning, I made up my mind (and hadn't told anyone even my wife) to tell Mason Lone Oak that I planned to accept the call to the Hillsboro church on the Monday night after the brotherhood meeting. I asked for and received a formal letter from the Hillsboro church, which I had in my briefcase.

On that particular Sunday, the members had left the church after the morning services. All but Sis Ora Lee Barnett, who lived about three doors from the church, she came back. My sermon was meant to be a farewell sermon though I said nothing about leaving. I was going to mention this at the next business meeting, Monday night. When she walked into the office, tears were running down her cheeks, and she said, "Pastor, don't leave us." I wondered, "How did she know?" I had just made up my mind that morning and had not discussed my plans with anybody. I just stood and looked at her; I didn't ask her how she knew. She said, "We going to do better, if you don't leave us." I picked up my briefcase and started to walk out the door with her following close behind me, crying all the way. I said, "I'll consider staying," and went to my car. Experiencing what I did with Sis Barnett, I decided to turn down the call to pastor the church in Hillsboro. That position would have required a move from San Marcos to Hillsboro but my wife was against that because of all we had done to build a life in our town.

When I returned to Lockhart the next Sunday, I found that Mason Lone Oak had received a letter from Hillsboro inviting us to come for a service at 4:00 clock. Somehow after the service, Mason Lone Oak members learned that the Hillsboro church had tried to call me to be their pastor. Mason Lone Oak offered to pay me a salary of $55 a week. When I left after 24 years, I was receiving about $80 a week. I wasn't suffering though; God was blessing me. I was working at Gary Job Corps at night, and running my plumbing business by day.

CHAPTER 15

"Entering Politics from the 1950's through the 1990's"

*

'SURPRISED' HARDLY DESCRIBES how I felt when I received the call asking me to be present at the Southside Community Center, a center owned by the Methodist Church. I had no idea with whom I was talking and was more surprised when I learned it was Mr. H. Y. Price, the owner of the San Marcos Telephone Company. He wanted to acquaint me with the Board of Directors for the Center. I later received a letter inviting me to become a member of the Southside Community Center Board of Directors. I accepted this invitation and became a board member. Mr. Price was president of the board and assigned me to the Buildings and Grounds Committee, which was chaired by Mrs. Gene Scrutchin. I was the only black person on the board. Mrs. Scrutchin said, "This committee was given $21,000 five years ago to do some work. This was said at the first meeting we had after I became a member. I exclaimed, "Five years!" Mrs. Scrutchin heard me. She said, "Mr. Washington, I am putting you in charge of the maintenance work that this committee is charged to complete." Well, I learned something from that experience. If you talk too quick, you might find yourself with a job you didn't ask for. I was tasked to spend this $21,000 in the following manner: to have an 8 foot chain-linked fence placed around the property, to have a hard surface (black top) laid in the back yard of the Community Center, to have a hardwood maple floor installed, and to put a new roof on the building.

When all the work was finished, we were approximately $3,000 over our budget. The United Methodist Women's Board requested that the Center send someone to its meeting in New York City to explain the cost overruns.

Since I had been the projects manager for the Building and Grounds Committee, Mr. Price asked me to go to New York and respond to their questions. Mr. Price paid all my expenses for the trip to New York. Mrs. Nancy Ellis, who was also a board member at that time, attended the meeting in New York with me. Dr. Caruthers was presiding at the New York meeting. I was nervous because I had spent $3,000 dollars I wasn't supposed to spend. The Center had to adjust some of the classes held there because of the shortage. This really concerned me because I was the man who spent that money. Dr. Caruthers asked me to explain why the projects went over our budget. I said, "The five-year delay between the time the money was set aside for the work and the time the work was actually done resulted in higher than expected costs of materials and labor." I also told, "The condition of the roof had deteriorated during the five years of delay, making the work more expensive." Dr. Caruthers said, "Mr. Washington, you don't have to say anything else." I didn't get a chance to finish giving my report. The women in the meeting didn't have any questions. He accepted that explanation without further discussion. I can't tell you how nervous I was up there in New York, a Baptist spending $3,000 of Methodist money! It was a scary moment to me.

* * *

I was elected president of the Southside Community Center at the next meeting in October of 1960 or 1961. When I took office in January of that year, I discovered that the previous president had already spent all of the operating funds. He talked against me being elected and didn't want me on the committee at all. He was a Mexican and had served his maximum term. He wanted to put in another Mexican on the board but Mr. Price wanted me in that position and helped me out. We had classes to run for the Mexican and white people to help them keep up in their public schools. The teachers were student teachers from the University. Not having money now to run the classes, Mr. Price asked me to go to various businesses in town explaining our situation and to ask for donations. These businesses contributed enough money for the Center to operate its programs until June or July when the Methodist Women released money for the next fiscal year. I served two three-year terms as President of the Board. About a month before I was due to go off the board at Southside, we began to notice a foul odor in the building. We looked all over the building, but we couldn't find the source of the odor. When the board had decided to install some commodes for the little children, we discovered a trap door in one of the closets. When we opened the trap door, we found out the source of the odor. The building had settled, and the old caste iron sewer pipe had broken, allowing the sewage to flow under the floor. By the time we were ready to replace the broken pipe and install the commodes, my term on the board had expired, making it possible for the board to hire me without the conflicts of interest concern. Because gravel covered the ground underneath the floor, it was not soaking wet or muddy. I had to go under the floor to see what work needed to be done. In order to let the space under the floor dry out, we closed the restrooms. People who came to the Center had to use the restrooms at a gas station next door until the repairs were completed.

I rented a compressor and an air hammer to cut about four or five inches out of the cement beam to get to the broken pipe. A Mexican man named Pineda crawled under that building and operated the air hammer in the evenings after he left his day job at Gary. He had worked for me in my plumbing business before. We broke out one of the little ground-level windows that opened to the space under the floor and shoved the hammer through the hole. It took Mr. Pineda about three evenings to cut out enough cement to allow me to install the new pipe. He had to be very careful because we didn't want to crack the support beam. We had to dig a 25-foot ditch by hand in the yard because we didn't want to break the pipe again. It took us about three weeks to finish that job. We installed schedule 40 PVC pipe under the floor and in the yard.

* * *

Over the years after this experience, I served on a number of local and state boards and commissions. My politics included becoming the finance officer for the Community Action Board, secretary of the board, and president of the board for two terms. I served on the San Marcos Consolidated Independent School District board for four three-year terms. I ran unopposed in my last two elections. A white man named Bobby Dupree was appointed to the board to fill the seat of a man who was forced to resign because of statements he made in the hearing of a newspaper reporter. Bobby developed health problems and had to resign from his seat; however, he ran against me when my first term expired. He thought he had a good chance to defeat me, but he didn't even come close. During the campaign, I participated in forums sponsored by the

League of Women Voters in my second election campaign. Mrs. Wynette Barton was my campaign manager during my second run for the seat. I was one of the organizers of the Child Welfare Board of Hays County and served on the City of San Marcos Planning and Zoning Commission for 12 years.

* * *

While a member of the Community Action Board, I purchased two buildings for head start programs, one building in San Marcos now known as the *A Washington Child Development Center,* and a building in Lockhart, TX. I signed all of the payroll checks for employees in nine counties. I remember the day I was involved in a minor car wreck on my way to sign checks at the Community Action Office. When I got to the intersection of MLK and Mitchell, I made a left turn in the path of an oncoming vehicle. I was in a hurry, and I just didn't see the other car until it was too late. It messed my car up pretty bad. The police were called. They arrived at the accident, and I talked to them for a few minutes and walked up the street to the Community Action Office (a block from the accident) to sign the payroll checks. I didn't have time to wait for the tow truck to move my vehicle. Payroll checks for the employees in nine counties were signed every other week on Wednesdays, and employees were paid Fridays.

When I became the Community Action Board President, employees were being paid every week. It was hard to get an accurate payroll in such a short period of time. Some employees were not getting paid what they were supposed to and others were overpaid. So, I decided to change the payroll schedule from weekly to every two weeks. I signed checks for between 200 and 600 employees. On most Wednesdays, I would start signing checks at 10:00 in the morning and finish up around 1:00, after lunch. I had to sign checks for workers in the Weatherization Program, Head Start (Kyle, Blanco, Lockhart, Hayes for the two Head Starts in San Marcos, Prairie Lea, Luling, etc.). Each of the Head Start programs employed six to eight people. We paid the transportation for the staff in San Marcos, Lockhart, Luling, and Blanco; each community ran four or five vehicles.

When I first started on the board, some members tried to persuade me to get a signature stamp so that I wouldn't have to come in to sign the checks. I said, "No!" I couldn't trust that stamp would only be in my hand.

In the beginning we were dispensing six million dollars in government funds to operate the Community Action programs in three counties. By the time my tenure ended we were dispensing $600 million in nine counties. I was scared somebody would get a hold of that stamp and put my signature on the wrong thing. I made sure those checks passed through *my* hands. I didn't want to mess up the government's money. For fourteen years, I was in charge of finance for the Community Action, and I wanted to make sure all of the checks were legitimate.

* * *

I think this is a good time to talk about my family and how they felt about all this, you see I was involved in everything I could get my hands on and busier than a one-armed paper hanger! Maybe you are thinking this had a great affect on them. Yet, I heard no grumbling about my involvement in anything; but of course, I wasn't home much. My wife had always accepted everything I did as it was for the family. She knew my heart was in making a better life for my kids, my wife, my church and my community. You have a better understanding now of my situation here... I was a husband, father, pastor, and businessman and community leader; therefore, my three children did not get a lot of my time because of my many activities. I had learned a short poem as a child that really stuck by me and by which I conducted my life:

> "If a task is once begun
> Never leave it till it's done.
> Be the labor great or small
> Do it well or not at all."

I loved each one of my children and while I did not give them a quantity of time I gave them quality time whenever I could. I did my best to attend their football games, other sports events or whatever they did. However I never attended their debates with other schools because they always occurred during my most busy work time. My daughter Mabeleen was in the Royal Guard at school and well known on the volleyball team, and I supported her in that. Sam was on the football team and ran track. I supported him in both. Willie was in the high school band, and I supported him in that activity. My children knew that they could talk to me whenever they got ready, regardless of where I was working or what I was doing, I was always available for my children but when they approached me while I was with a customer, they never butted in but waited until I was finished talking. They had the best manners and way about them. I can't take credit for that because that was their mother's doing. Rosa Mae was the disciplinarian in the house. There was never was a time we had to go to the school because of a discipline problem with my children while the schools were segregated. But believe me, I spent plenty of time for the other children in school after integration. My grandfather always taught me that the teacher had already got her education and I needed to accept that. Rosa Mae would pass this on to them, "That teacher has her education; now, you get yours." She would say to our children, "I'm telling you, if you get in trouble at school on your time, you will be in trouble with me when you get home. If I can't handle you, you are going to answer to your daddy!" This came from my telling her about how my grandfather handled me.

All the problems the children had would come through Sam. Even the problems that other kids had, they would go through Sam to get to me. He wanted me to hear it from him first. There was a time I remember that Professor Harris thought he caught Sam smoking in school. That was his deduction. What really happened was this: he caught a bunch of boys in the restroom at school and someone had been smoking. Sam was the last one to leave the restroom so the principal put it on him. Sam went across the street from the school to Mr. Kerr's store and called his mother. I happened to be home at the time. Sam gave me the details about what really happened. He was not smoking but he did not argue with the principal. While I was eating lunch a little later, the principal called.

As soon as I heard Professor Harris' voice on the phone I said, "I know you are calling me to tell that you caught Sam smoking."

He said, "How did you know, Rev. Washington? I said, "Sam told me." The conversation didn't go any further; I just let him know that I was aware of what had happened and that I would take care of it.

Now Sam was the kind of son who would even come to me when he got into trouble at home or wherever. He was a young boy when my wife and I lived with her Aunt Mary Mag. Sam and Mary Mag would get into conflicts constantly. Many times, I would just put him in the car and drive him around until we talked through the problem he was having with his aunt or whoever. I seldom corrected him in front of others. When we were alone we would discuss whatever situation he was facing. I don't know quite how to explain this, but in one way, Sam was one of the most dangerous children that I raised. Sam didn't play and I knew it, he took everything seriously. A boy lived next door who had a way of teasing Sam. He would tease Sam, then turn and run behind his house. He would peek around the corner yelling every kind of ugly thing he could think of. One day the boy came out of his house teasing Sam, and the next thing I heard was a woman scream, "Oh, Lord!" I ran outside to see what had happened and asked her. My neighbor Velma Davis was standing by her son who was on the ground knocked out cold and she said, "Samuel Lee hit Michael in the head with a rock!" I just picked the boy up and carried him and her to the hospital. Sam was about nine years old. When I came back from the hospital, I talked to Sam and discovered that Michael had been picking on him and running around the house. Michael was running and turned around to look back when Sam hit him with a rock. When Sam stops talking and starts grinning, you better get out of his way; you better watch out.

Even so, he earned quite a good reputation among the parents and other older people in the community. He was trusted you catch what I mean. When Sam became a teenager and learned to drive, many parents trusted their children to go to school functions with him. Barbara Green was more like a sister to Sam and would ask her father if she could go certain places, and he would say "Who you going with?" If she said Sammy Lee, then it was all right. People trusted Sam. The same was true of Helen Jackson Franks. Her parents would let her ride with Sammy, too. Later my son Sam would introduce Barbara to her future husband!

Sam was not alone in his serious personality because Willie didn't play around either. Once the schools integrated I remember an incident that happened during a band trip to a football game in Kerrville. Willie rode the bus with the band, and the wife and I went to Prairie Lea to pick up his girlfriend to bring her to the game. He intended to ride back with his girlfriend in my car. He was going to drive with my wife and me sitting in the back seat. He needed to turn in a note, though from his mother telling the school that he would be coming home from the game with his parents. This note had to be turned in at a certain time. Many parents would just pick up their children after games and bring them home. In doing this parents didn't have to go to the school to pick up their children. Like I said before, Mr. Lyons, the band director, had a certain time for band members to turn in these consent forms. Even though Willie had a note from his mother to come home with us after the game, he gave it to Mr. Lyons a minute or so after his deadline. Mr. Lyons just decided he would not allow Willie to come home with us because he had waited so late. After the game, I went to the bus to get Willie. As I walked around the bus, I heard a discussion; I knew my son's voice. I looked up, and there was Willie grabbing Mr. Lyons' collar and drawing back his hand to hit him. I reached up and caught Willie's hand to stop him from hitting the teacher. If I had not arrived at that moment, I believe Willie would have nailed Mr. Lyons. Mr. Lyons never said a word; he just looked at Willie as if he didn't believe what was happening. I asked them what was going on. Mr. Lyons said, "Willie, go on home with your Daddy." I didn't say anything to my wife about what had happened until later. We just got in the car and came home. When Willie dropped my wife and me off at home, he took his girlfriend back to Prairie Lea. Then I told my wife about the incident involving Willie and Mr. Lyons and needless to say, my wife was upset about it. We were concerned that Mr. Lyons would report the incident and Willie would be expelled from school. But we never heard anymore about it.

Oh, there was another incident where Willie and two of his white friends got into a little trouble at a track meet in San Marcos. They boarded the Luling school bus and began harassing the students. Really Willie and his friends had no business on that bus, so they were arrested and brought before a magistrate for harassing the Luling students. I was working at the old hospital at the time. Samuel came up there where I was working and told me what had happened to Willie and his friends. He said, "Daddy, Willie has been arrested for bothering kids on the Luling bus. The city cops got him." After delivering the information, Sam went on back to school. I got in my truck and went to the municipal court, which was located in the old fire station. When I walked in the courtroom, Judge Sutton had sentenced Willie and the other boys to the reform school. The parents of the other boys had not been informed about the charges against their sons. I reminded the Judge that he would have trouble on his hands if he sent those boys to reform school without consulting their parents. He had already sent for a car and driver to take the boys off to the house of detention. He told the sheriff who was standing there, "Go get the parents." After the other parents arrived, the judge dismissed the case and turned the boys over to the custody of their parents. Willie never showed any fear.

My daughter Mabeleen never got into situations like Willie's arrest. She was a different sort of girl. If she thought she had done something that didn't please her daddy, she was sick about it. She would sit around and cry if she thought she had displeased me. A lot of times she would do things that displeased me, but I wouldn't tell her directly. I would tell her mother and let Rosa talk to her. You know, even today, Mabeleen doesn't want to do anything that will displease her daddy. She was a 'Daddy's girl.' Why I remember the time she was to go visit a friend in another city a hundred miles away. It was her senior year in school. They knew each through the Association at church. At that time I was building two rooms onto my house and the floor in the back bedroom was not finished. Some of the boards were not nailed down. She happened to go in there and stepped on a board, fell through hitting her leg on a floor joist breaking her leg. The time came for her to go and her leg had healed up. I told her that the money we spent on her leg, was the money we had saved for her trip. I told her we would wait for another time. She looked at me and said, "Daddy, everything I have ever needed or wanted you supplied. Are you going to stop now?" That was it; I went straight to the bank and took out a loan so she could take her trip.

* * *

My children's mother had a powerful impact on their upbringing. She didn't do much whipping, but they knew that she didn't beg them to do what she wanted done. And she started training them at an early age to be obedient. My wife could also keep me in check. Sometimes I would get upset when customers wouldn't pay me. When I walked in the door, she could tell by the expression on my face that something was bothering me. She would give the children money to go to a movie in order to make time for us to discuss my problem alone. Our children never heard us discussing grown folks' business of no kind. Rosa Mae and I decided during our courtship that we would do everything in our power to make a good, stable home for our children. We did this you see, her father left when she was 3 years old and her mother died when she was 5. She grew up without her parents, and my father and mother never married, so my grandparents raised me until I was 12 years old. So, we made a commitment to each other to be good parents for our children.

Rosa Mae and I also raised our grandson, Sean Kevin Washington. We got him when he was four days old in 1968. We initially kept the baby so

Willie, Kevin's father, and his wife, Peggy could work at the University of Texas. I performed the marriage ceremony for them. When Willie and his wife divorced, we all agreed that Sean should stay with my wife and me. Sean had been with us all his life until then. Willie attended a trade school called Nixon Clay where he studied computers. My wife and I sent Sean to Wonderland School until he was old enough to attend public school. He was the only black student in the Wonderland Pre-School. You could be any age to attend, as long as you were potty trained. This cost us $90 a month, which was a lot of money at the time. My wife looked upon Sean as if he was her biological child. I sometimes worried that Sean's mother or father would come back and want to take him to live with one of them. I knew they would have a fight on their hands because Rosa Mae was not going to give him up.

When I ran for a seat on the San Marcos City Council, my opponent, Ted Breihan and I received the same number of votes in the general election. Before the run-off was held, somebody called my wife and told her that if I won the run-off, Sean wouldn't come home from school one day. Rosa Mae told me that if I ever ran for another public office in this city, I would have to find another wife.

She said, "I'm not going to have the safety of my children jeopardized for you to hold a public office. It's just not worth the risk." Rosa Mae was crazy about Sean.

We never had any disciplinary problems with Sean at school or at home. On one occasion though, Mr. Lyon's, always measured Sean against his dad by saying, "Sean, your Daddy wouldn't have played it like that." Naturally this upset the boy. Sean discussed the problem with me, and I went to the school and talked with the band director. Now, Willie was a natural musician. He could play drums, bass, guitar, and saxophone. Sean did not like music that much and liked being compared to his father even less. He graduated from Southwest Texas State University in 1991.

* * *

Eventually in May 1994, the Head Start Program of Community Action, Inc. Hays, Caldwell and Blanco counties dedicated the *A Washington Child Development Center* in recognition of my years of service to the community. I served on the Community Action, Inc. Board of Directors for 25 years, the San Marcos Consolidated Independent School District Board of

Trustees for 12 years, the Southside Community Center Board for six years, the Hays County Child Welfare Board for six years. While this chapter is primarily about my political involvements these didn't end here, but I will talk about that later.

In this first picture are my daughter Mabeleen and her husband Chad. Shown in the subsequent photo are members of my family who came down for the celebration . . .

CHAPTER 16

"The Eighties, more rough times but full of Change"

*

I ORGANIZED THE Christian Fellowship Union in 1955 or1956 and it was still going strong now. The purpose of this Union was to try to get the city together. Rev. Ludington, Pastor of 2nd Baptist was the driving force behind this Union. Initially the program was designed for just pastors and preachers. Then it was decided that we needed our wives to be part of us. That is how the name became the Christian Fellowship Union. Ludington was the president of this union for years. In 1956 I went to pastor Mason Lone Oak and I brought that church in to the same Union. The purpose of this fellowship was to give some unity to the black people of the city through the churches. We tried to educate the black people as they were not considered to be anything in San Marcos in these early years. It took all the churches together to give the blacks some sense of purpose and significance, and to encourage fellowship. We did not want anyone to be left out. We wanted to raise the standard of the black community. We also had a large Fellowship Choir directed by Grace Coleman Sanders. Although the Fellowship Choir was disbanded several years back and the churches no longer hold monthly fellowship services, the Christian Fellowship Union still brings ministers together in a spirit of cooperation. For 24 years I pastored Mason Lone Oak. This is how it happened that I left.

I had been to a business meeting at Mason Lone Oak on a Monday night. Three churches were holding a business meeting on that same night, Greater Bethel (which previously was known as 2nd Baptist), First Baptist and mine. Now when I returned home, my wife told me that one of the deacons from First Baptist had called wanting me to return his call. Greater Bethel also held a business meeting that Monday night, and word got out that both churches were considering calling me to pastor. It didn't take long for word to travel in a small town like San Marcos. This is how it really happened. The news got to the two other churches before the meetings had ended. Greater Bethel's pulpit committee found out that First Baptist was really considering a preacher from Conroe to fill the vacant pulpit, so that killed what they wanted do.

I received a report from both my first wife and Mrs. Annie Freeman that Mrs. Nelvia Burleson suggested to the members in the meeting at First Baptist, "I think we ought to call Rev. Washington. You know our building is in bad shape, already condemned and I believe if we call Rev. Washington, we'll get a new church." Mrs. Annie Freeman, who would later become my second wife, spoke up in support of Mrs. Burleson's suggestion. The members who were present agreed that the pulpit should be offered to me. It was at this point that Deacon Sam Nichols called my house from their church. My wife told him that I was not at home. As soon as I got home from Lockhart I called Deacon Nichols and he said "Rev. Washington, First Baptist called you tonight to be our pastor." I said, "Well, I should get a letter indicating that the church has called me." He said, "You will get a letter, but the members wanted me to call you tonight." I asked him to call a meeting for Thursday night to discuss this matter. After I finished talking with Deacon Nichols, I called John Barnett, Chairman of my Deacon Board in Lockhart and told him that I would be meeting with the deacons and members of First Baptist. He said, "Pastor, I'll do everything I can to keep you at Mason Lone Oak, but I won't do anything to help you leave." However, I accepted the call the serve as pastor of First Baptist (NBC) in May 1980, taking the pulpit on the second Sunday.

* * *

I have preached at several white churches in San Marcos. Just to mention some, I preached at Calvary Baptist Church, Westover Baptist, St. Mark's Episcopal Church, and the First Presbyterian Church (Rev. Conway Wharton was pastor at that time). I have never had problems with interracial support of my ministry. My fellowship with various churches had helped me to gain the support of whites and Mexican Americans during the times I ran for positions on the school board and city Planning and Zoning commission. I have always found white congregations in San Marcos to be very receptive to black preachers.

'Things that are hidden God bringeth to light'

REV. ALPHONSO WASHINGTON is a pastor of the Mason Lone Oak Baptist Church in Lockhart and a supervisor in the maintenance department at Gary Job Corps. A native of Washington, D.C., he was the first Black licensed plumber in San Marcos—a license gained after a long struggle. Rev. Washington has been an active leader in the community and serves on the Planning and Zoning Commission.

REV. A. WASHINGTON

"Roots" is one of what I believe to be many of the untold stories of early America which to my thinking should have appeared in the beginning of the American history book.

My grandfather, Phillip Washington, told me many stories with the same principle in body and ending. But it never went back to the arrival in this country from Africa.

I I also feel the people of America should know the real truth about the builders of our country.

Those black slaves brought here from Africa, against their will, yet they contributed as much labor, grief, fear, sorrow, sweat, blood and human lives as did any in the building of America.

For the sake of covering up shame, the history writers have robbed the black people of America of their input in making this country what it has been and what it is now. But the things that are hidden God bringeth forth to light. Job 28:11.

Soon after I accepted the call to pastor First Baptist Church (NBC), I had what I thought was my second heart attack in 1981. I was working at Gary Job Corps at the time. Rev. Bacon, who was pastor of Mt. Zion Baptist Church in Austin, heard that I was sick and announced this during the morning service. His entire brotherhood came to First Baptist to participate in my "Pastor's Anniversary service, although I was unable to attend the service due to my illness. After the service, the members of his brotherhood stopped by my house to have prayer with me. I'll never forget them for that lovely expression of kindness. Every year after that, this brotherhood would take part in my anniversary. According to Dr. Rogers, my second heart attack was not as severe as the first one.

* * *

The church was condemned. I found this out not long after accepting the pastorship to the church. God had already given me a plan or vision. Being a part of the city planning and zoning commission I asked for time to continue services before they closed the doors of the church. I asked the commission for time to meet the city's requirement to put the church in order. I knew I would need the support of the deacon board and the whole church. I brought to the church a plan that would require six people in the church to stand up for the debt incurred in order to make the renovations. The day of the meeting at the Austin Savings and Loan, only two people showed up, the chairman of the Trustee Board, Johnny Bratton and I. We, as a church had put up $900 to get this loan started. This money was now lost because four people did not show up for the meeting. This made me realize that I needed fresh men as officers in the church. Therefore, I chose five new men to put before the church as deacons: Robert Burleson, Wallace Cheatham, Israel Anderson, Robert Bratton, and Johnny Bratton and the church accepted all of them. Oh, the current deacons were against it but the church outvoted them. Let me tell you why I did this: we had deacons and trustees in our church all right, but they were old and set in their ways. They reached back 40 years or more in the history of the church. It was almost impossible to move them from their viewpoints, as they had become complacent. Their main complaint was that I did not put them on trial for four or five months.

I approached Robert Burleson in becoming a deacon when he came to pick up an organ at my house for the Juneteenth program at the Community Center. His deceased grandfather had been a deacon in the church, and his father was now both deacon and treasurer. Robert didn't give me a reply then, but he did the following Sunday in church. The other men I chose also agreed to serve. There was no time to wait for the men to go through a trial period. I needed young deacons now who would support the church's building plans. In order to teach and train these new deacons I structured my Wednesday night Bible Study around the responsibilities of deacons, to give them the scriptural background they needed to be effective in their work. Each of these young men turned out to be excellent deacons, and I never regretted choosing them to serve. Deacons Wallace Cheatham and Robert Burleson came to be powerful leaders in First Baptist. Willie Gaston Burleson never was the power that his son, Robert, came to be. Robert's grandfather was also named Robert, but he was never the leader in the church that the younger Robert became. Eventually, Robert Burleson was elected chairman of the deacon board, and he did an outstanding job.

* * *

First Baptist had $21,000 in the bank-building fund when I took over as pastor. They had been talking about building a new church before I went to pastor Mason Lone Oak, more than twenty-five years before then. A new building was necessary because the city wouldn't grant permits to renovate the church. The problems with the church ranged from the foundation to the roof, the heating and cooling, the water, restrooms, and electrical problems just to cover a few. There were just too many things to 'fix' to stay in the old building. We could not get a permit for the renovations without first having a parking area and then permits. They refused to give us the permits because we were already nearly blocking the street during church services. The church had been built when horse and buggies were in fashion. The addition of work crews would just congest the area too much. In addition, the parsonage needed a new roof, which cost around $1,900. This house was relatively new and we should not have had that problem after just twelve years.

We had fundraisers and donations that soon increased the bank balance to $41,000. We had several things going on at once. The church sold dinners, Hattie Nell Mack sold homemade cakes, and we had a building fund drive all of which brought the bank balance up to $61,000. During this very important growth period of the church I was teaching tithing. Some members had begun to tithe. I promised the church that if 60% of the church would tithe we could pay for the church in 10 years! But of course that never happened.

Wallace Cheatham came to a business meeting reporting that he had found a lot in a hundred year flood zone. The owner wanted $16,000 for the lot. I instructed him to go back to the owner and find out the lowest price the man would take for the lot. The following day Wallace called me and said, "I got the owner down to $14,500." I told him to call a Monday night meeting, which he did. We discovered at the meeting that the man was leaving that weekend for Michigan and he required the payment for the lot to be in cash. We had the money in the bank but it was tied up in CD's that would cause heavy penalties if it were withdrawn early. The church only had $5,000 in its checking account.

On Tuesday morning the Lord prompted me to call Mr. Price and I asked him if he would be coming to his office in town. He said, "No, I will be helping my wife at home. But if you need to talk to me, come out here." I was at his home in Kyle by six in the morning. When I got there he was in the kitchen with his wife. He saw me approaching the house through the glass doors. He said, "Let's go up here to the swimming pool." We sat down on the diving board and talked. I explained the situation concerning our desire to purchase this lot, and without hesitation or discussion regarding security or collateral, he wrote a check for $10,000 made out to the First Baptist Church, NBC. He already had his checkbook in his shirt pocket at six in the morning. Now that was God working in this situation. I came back home and called Deacon Johnny Bratton, chairman of the Trustee Board, and asked him to call a meeting of the church. Deacon Robert Bratton, Johnny's son was just as active in the church as his father at that time. At this Tuesday night meeting all the officers were there on time except me. When I walked in I spoke with everyone and went straight to the desk where Johnny was sitting. I laid the check from Mr. Price before him. He picked up the check and said, "Brethren, the pastor presents us with a check from H. Y. Price in the amount of $10, 000. We can now buy the land." I then instructed them to take the check to the bank to get the cash out to give the seller before Friday, and to get a receipt since we were paying him in cash. We bought the lot at the corner of Mitchell and Daily Streets in April. Now our building drive was really underway; things began to happen! By August we were able to repay Mr. Price the full amount plus 8% interest. He turned around and wrote us a check for the 8% interest, overpayment 'he felt, since he did not require interest when he initially gave the check. After we paid Mr. Price, our banks balance was down to $51,000.

At the time we were spending money getting blueprints and securing the contractors, the money began to flow out of our account. Deacon William Barnett's employer gave $10,000 for the building fund drive, bringing our total bank balance to about $56,500. Tex Hughson made a donation, also. He was a pitcher for the Boston Red Sox. Once people found out we had bought the land and paid cash for it, the money started coming in to support our efforts.

There were a number of businessmen that I had confided in concerning the church. Mr. Price, the Honorable William Crook (Ambassador to India during Lyndon Johnson's presidency), and Garland Warren (owner of the Sac & Pac convenience stores), and other local businessmen told me not to build the church because the economy was in no shape for such a big project. These men were concerned about the interest rates, labor costs, and other financial considerations. I valued their judgment but the Lord had told me to build. This was my answer to them. Once the building project had begun, they made generous donations.

One of Robert's jobs was with Gulf Gas Company, hauling gas for them. He also worked for the theatre at night and was a security guard at Gary Job Corps. He died after being sick about six months or slightly more with a work related illness from his Gulf Gas job. I had no problems with the church while he lived but soon after his death, it seemed things began to get out of hand.

* * *

Robert Burleson's Daddy, Deacon Gaston Burleson, Deacon William Barnett, and Deacon Lloyd White were all opposed to the building project. Rev. Jack Rector, Moderator of the Guadalupe Missionary Baptist District, was opposed to my plan to build a new church. Knowing my position on the Planning and Zoning Commission he wanted me to pressure the City to grant us a permit to renovate the old church. This man came from Dallas to San Antonio and felt I should do as he did with his church. He was able to buy up all the homes around his condemned church and felt that I should do the same. He was in a big city and I was not. He had built a $2 million building-Antioch Baptist Church.

We went through many trials beginning in the blueprint stage. I had to get a blueprint that would work in a flood zone because we had already bought the land in a 100-year flood zone, according to the city.

We went through a series of blueprints that failed to work for various reasons the most important being our situation in the flood zone. We eventually found a contractor who really wanted to build the church for us. He told us he knew a man in San Antonio who would revise the plan we had prepared for us by an Indian architect at the cost of $200.00. This plan was not suitable for our situation but the man in San Antonio would revise this plan to fit the city and condition requirements. The church agreed to let this architect revise the plan for the building. The contractor was ready to build now! After the church was built I kept those plans for years, but after I left First Baptist Church, I got rid of them. This young contractor was experienced in just about every area except building a church. He was seriously interested in obtaining this experience and was excited to work with us.

Soon after we bought the land, we had a ceremony to celebrate our ground-breaking for the new church it was March of 1986. The city and the county were both involved in the ground breaking. I had specific ideas about how the church would be involved with the contractor and set up a committee of people for the building of the church. This committee had only one person who would talk to the contractor. I set it up this way because I was a contractor myself and having too many people trying to tell a contractor what to do would make a big mess! I chose Deacon Johnny Bratton to be the only person to work with the contractor because he was also a Trustee for the church. Unfortunately Johnny took sick with cancer and died rather quickly. His funeral became the first held in the new church. At this time my wife had just learned she had cancer; more about that later. It was a rough time because we had so many deaths in a short period of time.

I then appointed Deacon Wallace Cheatham to take over the responsibility that Johnny had on the committee. He actually took over when Johnny first became sick and the doctors told him he didn't have long. These two men, Robert and Wallace took on the responsibility and did an excellent job, I wish I had the words to say how proud I was of the manner in which they both accepted this responsibility and carried it out. Many times I would say, "If Moses had had a committee, the Israelites would still be in Egypt." I learned many years ago that everybody's job is nobody's job. For this reason I always put one person in charge of carrying out the will of the committee.

When we reached the stage that where we needed to find a plumbing contractor, the cheapest one was found in San Antonio. He wanted $35,000 to put in the plumbing; he was the cheapest bid we got! I advised the church that I would do the plumbing and save them a lot of money. I knew I could do it much cheaper. Because I was a contractor myself I allowed the church the advantage of the wholesale prices I received for the materials needed to do the work. I was able to get the work done quickly and with the best quality possible. I did the job for $6,500. We tried hard to get pews from a store in Austin that sold used church furnishings, but we couldn't find what we wanted. After discussing this problem, we decided to have our pews custom made choosing Sam's in Waco who built the new church pews to our specifications.

* * *

The Lord blessed us with money rolling in from outside the church. We had a money market account and a checking account. We always had enough money in the checking account to pay our bills on time. The *Friends of First Baptist* would mail us checks regularly to help cover our expenses. When we first started, we already found the windows we were going to put the church would require more money than allotted for them. We consulted the contractor about the additional charges and he suggested that we could cut off six feet from the fellowship hall to accommodate this change. The cement forms had been set up but no cement had been poured. Deacons Robert Burleson, Wallace Cheatham, and Johnnie Bratton decided to keep the old pulpit furniture. When the church was under construction, I was having bad sinus trouble, so I asked them not to put ceiling fans in the choir stand.

* * *

The Dean of Guadeloupe College was Reverend Hall. He was also the pastor of Trinity Baptist Church so I invited him to come and preach our dedication service in November 1986. We had many local dignitaries present at the dedication. Among those present at this service was Ambassador William Crook, president of the San Marcos Baptist Academy, was a regular contributor to First Baptist. I became pastor in May 1980 and served until November of 1989. During this time I named Sis Helen Jackson Franks to the trustee board, making her the first woman to serve as a Trustee and she still serves to this day. Sis Franks started the annual Taste Tea fundraiser. Right before I left the church a dispute arose regarding church policy that would eventually cause me to resign as pastor. I choose not to go into detail in an effort not to re-open old wounds. At our regular business meeting we discussed the matter of the Taste Tea, and I could see that the congregation was divided. I had been preaching and teaching tithing as God's way of financing the church. So I was completely against this business of having a Taste Tea event as the principle way to raise money. Many of the members did not want to tithe but would rather hold something like this to raise money to support the church. Seeing the division in the church over this matter, I decided to resign as pastor. I did not want to be pastor of a church, preaching and teaching one thing and the members doing another, outside the vision of their pastor. A vote was taken to determine how many members were in favor of terminating my service as pastor. The vote was evenly divided between those who wanted me to remain as pastor and those who favored my resignation. To avoid splitting the congregation, I submitted my resignation again at that meeting, the first Monday after the first Sunday in November 1989.

CHAPTER 17

1985-86
"The Austin Diagnostic Clinic"

*

THIS MOST IMPORTANT woman in my life at this time was my wife, Rosa Mae. She deserves a chapter all to herself. She became seriously ill in early 1986, before work on the new church began. But I remember the first sickness that she had was right after we married in 1943. She was employed by Southwest Texas State (SWT) Teachers College when after work while walking home she collapsed on North Guadeloupe Street. Someone saw her lying on the side of the street, called the ambulance who took her to the hospital. I was still a soldier and when I came home from the base and couldn't find her, I called the hospital to see if she was there; I didn't know where else to look for her. She had worked nine months at SWT earning only $200 a month. The hospital bill we received was $1,700. However, Travelers Insurance paid the bill; thank the Lord. I wouldn't let her go back to work after that illness because she was far more valuable to me as a housewife than the piddling amount she made a month at the college.

Her second serious illness came after our third child was born. It was discovered that she had cancerous uterine tumors. Dr. Sowell, our family doctor diagnosed the case, but he was not a surgeon. Dr. White was recommended to do the surgery. It was around 1950. Another illness occurred sometime later. Dr. Sowell had died right after her surgery and we got a new family doctor, Dr. Rogers. He diagnosed the illness that happened following her surgery in 1950. Around 1966 Dr. Rogers sent Rosa Mae to a doctor from Lockhart who served on the staff of the Austin Diagnostic Clinic. This doctor examined Rosa Mae and confirmed the earlier diagnoses. However, he said he would not attempt the surgery without the help of two other specialists in California. The morning of the surgery at Brackenridge Hospital, Dr. Rogers, the doctor from Lockhart and the specialists from California took Rosa into the operating room at 7:00 a.m. When she came out of the recovery room, it was 9:00 p.m. that evening. I personally do not believe that she ever fully recovered from this surgery. So much so, that I stopped her from ironing my shirts, something she loved to do and at which she excelled. I started sending my shirts to the laundry. I just didn't want her to do that extra work.

* * *

Rosa Mae's next serious illness occurred August 1985. Dr. Rogers thought she was experiencing heart problems at this time and sent her to see Dr. Ken Smith, a heart specialist. It was November 1985. It was not long before Dr. Smith uncovered that she had a heart condition. After caring for her heart problems a while, on the 11th of January 1986, he found out that my Rosa Mae had breast cancer. It seriously bothered me that Dr. Rogers had been seeing her every other week, running her through all kinds of tests running up all kinds of bills and never discovered the cancer knowing she had a cancer history. Dr. Smith also noticed that the medication for the heart condition was not working as it should have worked. So, he made arrangements for Rosa Mae to have a thorough physical examination in an effort to find out why the heart medication was not working properly.

When the physical was completed, Dr. Rogers happened to be in radiology at hospital. He seemed surprised when he saw me there and asked why I was there. I told him, "Dr. Smith had ordered some x-rays for Rosa Mae." He said, "Would you mind if I look at Rosa Mae's x-rays?" I told him he would need to get Dr. Smith's permission. He said he would talk to Dr. Smith, but he wanted my approval first. I said, "You been doctoring on her all these years; I don't mind if you look at the x-rays." Dr. Rogers called Dr. Smith and got his permission to view them. Now Dr. Rogers was a white man but when he looked at the x-rays he turned white, really white like he was bleached! He wanted to talk to Dr. Smith but privately.

When he returned to me, he said, "Dr. Smith wants you to bring Rosa Mae to his office right now." I was completely shocked having seen his complexion change and then when he came back and said what he did we both felt something was up but we were not sure what it was. My wife didn't say anything during the drive back to Dr. Smith's office.

When we arrived at Dr. Smith's office, he told Rosa "Let me check your left breast." He said "That's it!" I said, "What do you mean?" He said, "She has breast cancer." I asked Dr. Smith to call our daughter, Mabeleen, who was in Hubbard Hospital, O'Hare Nursing and Doctors School, Nashville TN working as a registered nurse. He called her and talked with her. Then Mabeleen asked to speak with me. She said, "Daddy, whatever those doctors want to do, let them do it." Dr. Smith went on to say that "according to what Dr. Rogers told me about the x-rays, I have to do something about this now." He said, "I want you to take her to the Diagnostic Clinic" in Austin. The next day, I took Rosa Mae for the second time to the clinic. The doctors at the Clinic took some new x-rays, but they never let me see them. I didn't ask to see them because I wouldn't have known what I was looking at anyway.

By the next month, February—Mabeleen came home from TN to see her mother, Samuel, came from Washington, D.C., and he and his sister arrived in San Marcos at the same time. Mabeleen wanted to see the x-rays, so I took her out to Dr. Rogers' office. He did not have them there so I took Mabeleen to the Clinic in Austin. Rosa had been taking chemotherapy and was undergoing radiation treatments at the Clinic in Austin. When Mabeleen saw her mother's x-rays at the clinic she told me on the trip back to San Marcos, "Daddy, I know you don't want to hear what I have to tell you, but if I had seen those x-rays before the doctors started giving Mama chemotherapy and radiation treatments, I would have told you to forget about the treatments." She was trying to prepare me then for what she knew what was soon to be coming down the road. After that she and Sam returned to their respective homes and jobs.

* * *

On Rosa Mae's last day she asked me to get something for her. When I brought it, she said, "I have to go to the bathroom." I had no idea that she was dying. I lifted her out of bed and put her in her wheel chair. I got her almost to the bathroom when I noticed that she had begun to lean to one side as if she was falling asleep. I said "Wake up baby; don't give up." She said, "No, don't give up." Those were her last words. I took her out of the wheel chair and put her back in the bed and called EMS. She died on the first day of April 1986. I also called Georgia Cheatham and my grandson, Kevin, who was a senior at San Marcos High School.

After his mother was buried, Sam stayed until August. He went back briefly to Washington to take care of some business, but came back to San Marcos and stayed with Sean and me. At this time, he returned to Washington for about a week, and then came back to San Marcos and stayed until October. Sam worked on my account books for my plumbing business and brought them up to date. He then showed my grandson, Sean, how to keep the books. Actually, Sean had already been helping my wife with the books before she became ill. My wife had learned from my daughter. When Mabeleen was in high school, she started to keep the books. Later, Mabeleen took a job as secretary in the maintenance department at the San Marcos Baptist Academy where I was in charge of plumbing. That's where she learned how to keep books. She also ordered my plumbing supplies for my business and for the Academy, a job she was quite capable of performing.

CHAPTER 18

"Changes in Both my Church and Personal life"

*

A YEAR AND four months after the death of my first wife, I married Mrs. Annie Freeman, a widow and member of First Baptist. We had served in church together since 1943 when I first arrived in San Marcos for 12 years. When I met her, she was an usher at there and her husband, Willie, was a deacon. During the time I pastored Mason Lone Oak and subsequently came to pastor First Baptist we were still acquainted. She had become a widow and built a new home shortly before Rosa Mae died. Mrs. Freeman called me to fix some problems she had with leaks in her new house. I mention that this happened prior to my first wife's death because these calls began sometime before Rosa Mae died. I did not want to respond to her first 2 a.m. call but Rosa Mae insisted that I go because she was a widow and needed help with her plumbing and I was a plumber. As a result of the frequent calls to work on her plumbing after my first wife died, we developed a closer relationship. We were married on July 3, 1987. My daughter Mabeleen and Mrs. Freeman's daughter Josephine decorated the church for the wedding. We had a good marriage for about four months, but we began to realize that we were incompatible. It is funny how you can think you know a person because you served in the same church for 25 years or so, and are acquainted 20 more years, but I really didn't know her at all. She certainly didn't know me nor understand my call to preach and pastor. Our children attended school together. My children say they tried to warn me against marrying Mrs. Freeman, but I don't remember that part. They were quite right, though! During this brief marriage we took a trip to California to visit her children. She intended for me to leave the church. That was not going to happen. I left her on the 15th day of January 1991; by April, she got the divorce. However, my commitment and dedication to her caused me to remain in close touch with her, and I took care of her when she became sick and disabled. Even after the divorce, I maintained a friendly relationship with Mrs. Freeman's children. I know that each of my wives came into my life in His perfect time and for God's purpose to be full-filled. Let me explain . . .

* * *

In the second year after Mrs. Freeman and I were married I began visiting Sledge Chapel Baptist Church in Kyle, and moved my membership there where Rev. Wade was the pastor. Sledge Chapel was her home church as a child. But by this time I knew without a doubt that Mrs. Freeman did not want me to pastor any church anywhere! She really wanted me to stay in California. The main cause of our problems stemmed from her extreme jealousy. However in May of 1990, I received a call from Rev. Wade asking me to attend a special called meeting at the church. I did not know that Rev. Wade had planned to resign at that meeting. He had been named one of the associate ministers at Mount Zion First Baptist Church in San Antonio, where Rev. Black was senior pastor. Rev. Black had assigned Rev. Wade to oversee the church's outreach ministry to the sick and shut-ins, with his main responsibility being to visit nursing homes, hospitals, and such. I knew that Rev. Wade had been involved with the outreach ministry in San Antonio for approximately a year before he resigned from Sledge Chapel. Apparently, handling both jobs—serving as pastor of Sledge Chapel and working as the Outreach Minister for Mount Zion First Baptist—was becoming too demanding.

Rev. Wade told the congregation, "I am resigning, but I am leaving you in good hands." He walked around behind the chair where I was sitting and pointed to me as he made that statement. I knew exactly what he was doing. I caught him pointing toward me. Now I didn't see this but my wife did. The church called me to serve as pastor that same night, but I didn't accept the call until July. I preached as an interim pastor every Sunday. I wanted the congregation to have time to make up their mind as to whether or not they really wanted me. And to be honest about it, I was not ready to take on that responsibility. I needed more time to come to terms with my separation from First Baptist (NBC) where I had worked hard moving the church and building the new one and pastored more than 9 years. I served as pastor for two and a half years at Sledge Chapel, even though Mrs. Freeman and I had separated. During this tenure I became knowledgeable of the Southern Baptist Convention.

Rev. Wade had been trying for about two years to get Sledge Chapel into the Southern Baptist Convention (SBC). Some of the members supported his efforts to join, but other members were opposed to seeking membership in this predominantly all white convention. I was able to get the majority of the members to support the plan to join the (SBC). The following October, the SBC accepted membership applications from churches.

The Southern Baptist Convention requested that I go to the white First Baptist Church in Seguin to attend classes in evangelical ministry. I had to pay $132 for the course, but Sister Sneed and Sister Manning who came with me, did not have to pay. After we finished the course, I was supposed to establish evangelical training at Sledge Chapel, but I couldn't get enough students to make the program work. In April of 1991, I received my diploma from the Evangelical School.

* * *

The doctors thought that I had prostate cancer in April 1992. I later found out that I had a tumor, but it was not cancerous. Sledge Chapel heard the rumor about my health problems and began to worry about the status of my health. I became the talk of the church and their concern that I would become a burden to the church. Some members believed that I had been diagnosed with prostate cancer even though this was not true. The talk continued so much so that in June, the rumors came to my attention. To put the church at ease, I thought it would be best for me to resign, and I did so in that same month. Dr. Rogers sent me to Audie Murphy Hospital to be examined. He sent my x-rays to the doctors in San Antonio, but I don't think they even looked at them. On the same day that I was admitted, the doctors at Audie Murphy started to take their own x-rays. After they read their in-house x-rays, the doctors told me that I had tumors, but they were not malignant. I was in the hospital for two days for the tests. In July, I went back to Audie Murphy for the surgery and stayed in the hospital about eleven or twelve days.

When I was released from the hospital, I stayed at home during my convalescence period. It was a strange time for me as I didn't go to church for nearly a year. I began attending church at First Baptist (NBC) in December of 1992. Rev. Franklin preached on the second Sunday that month. I returned a couple of Sundays later. I came back on the night that he accepted the call to pastor; it was a Thursday night. I joined First Baptist that night. So, I was the first member that Rev. Franklin took in as pastor. I felt that I had been out of church long enough. I had observed Rev. Franklin, and I believed he was a pastor I could follow. After church was dismissed, Deacon Edgar Sayles came to me and said, "I'm proud of you, and I am glad that you have come back to First Baptist."

* * *

Rev. Franklin was a military man who had spent 23 years or so in the US Army. He really advanced in rank quickly. He was not retired when he took on the pastorship of the church and lived in Killeen TX and was stationed at Fort Hood Army Base. In July he retired and moved to San Marcos to live in the parsonage. This was a difficult move because he lived in a big fine house; top of the line everything. The parsonage was a far cry from what he was used to. Edgar Sayles and I had to redo some major carpenter work and plumbing work before he and his family could move in. He had rented his home in Killeen. When they moved into the parsonage he came with his wife and daughter. They had just lost 2 sons. One died in childbirth and the other, a teenager had taken his mother's car and was killed in an accident.

He pastored First Baptist about nine years after he had contracted Agent Orange, a war disease from which he suffered until his death in November 2001.

While I was at First Baptist in 1996 I began to have more health problems. These problems followed one of the most strenuous jobs I worked in my latter years. In the early part of the year 1995, Kyev Tatum challenged the city of San Marcos to give him the old Dunbar school building, which had been moved and set up on a city lot for years, outside the city limits by the sewer plant. His purpose in moving this building back within the city limits was to make the 'Mitchell Center', to be used for civil work in the city. It was meant to help the children failing in school, house the NAACP meetings, and the WOW (Words Of Wisdom) meetings just to name a few. This he accomplished by getting the city to give him several lots from which condemned houses had been removed. Once the building was moved to the Valley Street location it needed work to make it useable. The overall size of the revised building would contain two bathrooms, a large kitchen, a laundry room, three classrooms and two offices. This was a huge building, an undertaking in which I did all the plumbing and gas work for the heating and cooling by myself, and at the age of 82. I had to hook up the drinking fountain and a few other small things when I took sick and could not finish. Someone else finished the loose ends of this project.

I was living in my house on Texas Avenue, along with one of my granddaughters, Rochelle and her son, Tevin, when I found out I had pneumonia. I went to Audie Murphy hospital on the 31st of December 1995. As I was about to be released, Dr. Easton came around picking up my chart from the foot of the bed. She saw that while in the hospital I had steadily lost weight. She wanted to know why I was losing weight every day for seven days. She canceled my discharge and started to research this problem. I was there a whole month while they were running tests to find the problem. In February 1996 she found the problem to be lung cancer. She ordered an immediate operation on my lung. This ended up taking three surgeries to complete.

* * *

I was put on a portable oxygen tank to assist my breathing. My recovery time was approximated to be a year and a half. I returned home from the hospital on the 6th of March 1996. I called my friend Dr. Verna Henson from the hospital and told her I was coming home. She came to the house to visit me and was appalled when she saw the living conditions in the house. She got to the house about one hour after me. I was taken straight to my bedroom so I could be hooked up to the oxygen and had not seen the house at all. When Verna arrived, she saw the state of things that I had not seen. She immediately desired to help me get things in the house straight. I begged her not to do anything because my granddaughter would take care of it when she got home. Within about a month, I began to learn what kind of financial shape I was now in. None of my bills were paid the whole time I was in the hospital from November through March and April. Rochelle had written her cousin Brian Melton to ask for money to try to pay some of the bills. I had no checks at all and yet no bills were paid. I never knew what those checks were written for. Brian called his mother, Mabeleen in California and she called my son Sam in Virginia. They decided to meet at my house immediately. Sam arrived first and Mabeleen got there later in the day. Now it is July 1996 and my children are in the midst of utter chaos regarding my granddaughters. My children had got me a place in CAMLU (an assisted living apartment franchise of owned by Cambell and Lundt, I believe) at the next open room. Brian and Kendra came on the 29th of July along with the American Legion commander, Tom Tvrdik and his two sons and another person from the legion. They loaded up all my furniture and stuff emptying the house completely. I had already given what I could to whoever wanted whatever. A few of my things were loaded on my truck to be carried to Brian's house in Houston. The first of August I flew to my son Willies' house in Nashville TN. I remained at Willie and Tish's house all of August and September. I received a phone call from Sam saying that my place at CAMLU would be ready on the first of October. My truck had been left at Brian's in Houston. I flew from TN to Houston shortly upon hearing my room was ready. Sam met me in Houston and drove me back to San Marcos. The circumstances that had continued to develop caused me to have sell my home on Texas Avenue and move. When I bought the property on Texas Avenue, it was outside of the city limits. However, as the city grew, my property was eventually taken in by the city and zoned industrial. My office and shop for my plumbing business was attached to my house, so I was allowed to maintain my residence even though the street was no longer zoned residential. They (the city) couldn't run me away from the property. But when I retired from the plumbing business, I knew I would eventually have to sell the property and relocate my residence. I owned another lot in the area, so I had planned to move my house to my other lot. After I got sick though, and went through what I had to when I returned home, I gave up the idea of moving the house.

During the time that I was in the hospital, my personal financial situation had deteriorated such that I found I was $35,000 in debt. My truck payments were several months behind, and I had some credit card bills that needed to be paid. The only way I could get that much money quickly was by selling my property. I was losing any hope of recovering financially because this situation was disastrous for me. Because the sale was so quick I lost even more money and was left destitute except for a few books, the clothes on my back and the help of my children. I had absolutely nothing. I knew that God would provide for me.

* * *

Now my being a diabetic was an additional problem. Mabeleen and Sam wanted me to move to a place where I would have assistance with my housekeeping and meals. They probably knew that I would have just eaten whatever I wanted. I could have lived much cheaper in a rented house or apartment, but I would have needed someone to come in and fix my meals. The CAMLU staff dietitian made sure that I ate according to my diet. Mabeleen had found CAMLU and paid the fee required to get my apartment. While some people may think this remarkable I was the only black resident of CAMLU, but I got along well with the other residents and the staff. I have never had any trouble relating to people of different races or ethnic groups. I just treat people the way I want to be treated and expect the same from them. Owning my own plumbing business was perhaps the greatest means for me to come in contact with many different kinds of people, not to mention my years of pastoring churches. I realized that the success of my business depended to a large degree on how I related to my customers and the success of my pastoring depended upon how I related to the members over which God had given me charge. Those many years of experience working with the public helped to make my adjustment to CAMLU easy, too. Soon after I moved there, I was elected president of the Residents Council. We met on the first Wednesday of the month to consider residential problems such as noise, menus, recreational activities, and other quality of life issues. When we received a complaint, the Council would take the matter to the management and see if a reasonable solution could be found. It was within a year that CAMLU was bought out by another company that already owned 93 retirement and assisted living centers just in Texas alone. The new name of our center would be Redwood Springs. During the six years I remained there I also taught a Bible study as part of my outreach ministry for First Baptist Church (NBC). I remained active as Senior Associate Minister of First Baptist, and I was active in the local American Legion Post as chaplain, while I resided at Redwood Springs. While I remained quite active, the main reason was that at my place I had four walls to look at. On the days I did not get out, I studied my bible and books, in case I needed a sermon in my pocket. I was almost always prepared should I be called to preach.

* * *

Life was about to take a dramatic turn for me. My grandson, Brian made a computer for me and showed me how to use it. The main purpose to **me** was writing or outlining my sermons but to **him**, I was going to learn how to keep in touch with everyone via something very new to me—*e-mail*! Now I know I mentioned this before, but new things were always exciting to me. I heard about how older people didn't like to learn new things but that just wasn't me. I loved new things. And I appreciated the time that he and my son Willie took with me. It did take time for them because until I was well versed in what I was doing, I was always causing something to go wrong that needed to be fixed. But finally we came to the part where I got online for the first time. It is hard to describe the feeling I got when I wrote and sent an email then got one back! Now that was really something! Mind you I was in my eighties. I never cared much for getting around the internet, emails were enough for me. To be able to instantly write and send a note or letter through an email was astonishing to me. I had no idea how important my grasping this technology would prove to be in the near future. But it was through this that my life was about to change dramatically! It was now the mid to late 90's and I was rolling along working my favorite thing—studying the bible!

I learned to use my computer along with the Bible study groups I was involved with. During this time I was listed in the U. S. Registry's 'Who's Who' Among Outstanding Americans™ 1994-1995 (ISBN 0-9360708-2-0), Who's Who Publications at 1000 Park Boulevard, Suite 209, Massapequa Park NY 11762. I am listed on page 454 as an Outstanding Master Plumber and Bible Teacher. How this came about I am unsure. I learned of it when they contacted me for a picture, which I did not send to them. Beginning my work with the computer initially required direct involvement with my son, Willie or grandson, Brian. Soon I was able to place a call and follow instructions to get myself out of some of the difficulties I encountered.

Christmas of 1994 I spent the holiday with my grandson, Brian in Houston TX. It was here that I learned that my grandson and son had planned to give me a computer but they had not quite finished building it from scratch. They wanted to give it to me while I was with Brian so he could explain how to use it. He gave me valuable lessons! I brought it home with me and immediately started practicing. I messed it up twice before I moved into CAMLU. In July of 1996 I carried my computer with me to my son's house in Nashville for him to fix. This computer was a Windows 95 and my son wanted me to have a more up to date computer and so he built me a Windows 98. I brought my computer with me from Nashville to CAMLU.

I started emailing some of the church members back in 1995 almost daily. It was so amazing to me that I could email one of them and get a response before I got away from the computer! After this move to the Retirement Center I added to my growing numbers in bible study groups. The assistant manager at CAMLU would now be the one to help me with my computer. He taught me how to use the computer to set up my bible studies and how to add a printer. Someone gave me an old printer that was modified to use with my computer. I was on my way now!

* * *

Over the next five or six years, I lived a happy life yet I was pretty much confined to the four walls of my room at Redwood Springs. There was a great deal of time afforded me to work with my computer and bible study. During this time I walked, working up to a mile a day. On Sunday's my dietician would always save my meal for when I got back. It was always after the meals had been served to the others. I carried a banana or two with me everywhere I went. Once my second wife and I separated in January and divorced in April 1991, I was considered quite a catch... eligible bachelor, if you catch what I mean. But "burnt children are afraid of fire'. I kept my distance for the most part. I maintained a very few close relationships.

The following Old Testament scripture became especially meaningful in a powerful way to me in my latter years. It comes from Haggai the prophet who wrote these prophetic words:

Haggai 2:5-9 "[This is] the promise I made to you when you came out of Egypt, and My Spirit is present among you; don't be afraid." 6 For the LORD of Hosts says this: "Once more, in a little while, I am going to shake the heavens and the earth, the sea and the dry land. 7 I will shake all the nations so that the treasures of all the nations will come, and I will fill this house with glory," says the LORD of Hosts. 8 "The silver and gold belong to Me"—the declaration of the LORD of Hosts. 9 "The final glory of this house will be greater than the first," says the LORD of Hosts. "I will provide peace in this place"—the declaration of the LORD of Hosts.

I could not imagine how this promise would come true in a way, and apply to me in my latter years. But each time God moved me from one place to another, it just kept on getting better and better.

CHAPTER 19

2001-Present
"Carry me back to old Virginia"

*

MAY 2 2000, my brother Rev. James Burrell, pastor of Swift Ford Baptist Church, passed on to glory! I found this out because my grandson Kevin, called to let me know and asked if I wanted to go. I said yes, and he paid my way, emailing me the itinerary. I stayed at my son, Sam's house in Falls Church VA. At James' funeral, on the service held in Manassas VA, I met the pastor of Mount Morris Baptist Church in Hume, VA, Rev. Lindsay O. Green. There were many preachers there that night but I was asked to speak on behalf of the family. It turned out that Rev. Green was married to my first cousin, once removed, Carolyn J. Green. She was the daughter of Henry and Frankie Washington Julius.

One year later I had the opportunity to attend the Washington Family Reunion, in Front Royal VA on July 7. This family reunion is always held on the 1st Saturday in July. I was able to get a plane ticket to Virginia and stayed with my brother William in Washington DC. We attended the Family Reunion and while there, Pastor Green came up to ask if I would come back in September and run the revival before their homecoming. My own pastor was sick at the time, suffering from Agent Orange so I told Pastor Green I would first check with my pastor and then let him know. When I returned to San Marcos I visited my pastor, Rev. Franklin at Audie Murphy Veterans Hospital in San Antonio TX. I told him of the invitation to preach revival in VA but that I had not answered, as I wanted to discuss it with him. When I told him he said, "The Lord called you to preach and don't ever turn down an invitation because of me." He had a whole lot of brothers in the Gospel who could fill in for him if I were unable. I called Pastor Green and told him all I needed was roundtrip transportation to VA. Pastor Green said, "We'll take care of that!" The revival was scheduled to run from September 17-22, 2001. I was excited about preaching at Mount Morris Baptist Church because my maternal great grandfather, Elder Cornelius Gaddis was the founder and first pastor. My grandfather that raised me, Elder Phillip Washington was the third pastor of this church. This was a great personal opportunity for me. Little did I know how great!

* * *

I am about to tell you an amazing story, the beginning of which I would learn after I arrived in Virginia. I was told that Pastor Green held his quarterly business meeting on July 21st after the Family Reunion in 2001. In the previous year, at the same business meeting in July, he had asked the church if someone would volunteer to take in a visiting minister and possibly their wife. The year before they had a minister who was put up at the hotel in town and it was quite expensive for the church. Deacon Robert Whitmore stood up and volunteered his residence. Deacon Whitmore was called home to God on August 27, 2000, about a month later. Now at the business meeting in July 2001, knowing that there was a possibility that I might be preaching revival for him, Pastor Green asked Sis Whitmore at the church meeting, if she would honor her deceased husband's offer. At this time she had her oldest daughter, Debra and son in law living with her, while in the process of relocating from Pennsylvania to Virginia. This made it suitable for her to accept Pastor Green's request, if need be. At this same business meeting Sis Whitmore was elected a delegate along with Sis Mildred Gaskins, the church clerk, to the Second National Ketoctan Baptist Association meeting in August. Carol Whitmore was also the church Secretary. Carol had requested a vacation time to begin on the last day of the Association, August 26th making it necessary to leave early—by noon. Pastor Green called her aside prior to her leaving the association and gave her a job to do before she left for vacation. She was tasked with finding my airline ticket online and getting all the information to me before she left.

Carol made the reservations and called me at their request that afternoon prior to leaving on her vacation. The purpose of her call was to put me at ease regarding my lodging and flight arrangements. Our conversation lasted approximately an hour. I'm going to say something here I hope you understand. I was attracted to Carol after the first moment I heard her voice. I would compare my feeling to Sis Whitmore's voice to

Elizabeth's response to Mary's pregnancy. The baby leapt in Elizabeth's womb. Well, I don't have a womb, but something quickened in my Spirit when I first heard her talk. She was completely unaware, and I was going to keep it that way. She tried to give me the flight schedule, but I asked if she had email. She agreed to email my itinerary to me. After exchanging email addresses, I decided that email would be the most convenient and cost effective means of maintaining contact with Carol.

I did not hear from Carol again until after she returned from her trip on September 9th 2001. Just two days before the country would suffer the shock of terrorist attacks on our nation. After September 11th and the tragedy that occurred that day, we shared many emails in preparation for my trip but most of our correspondence then focused on the terrorist attacks in NY and Washington DC, both of us having family working in Washington. This was an intense time for both our families. I have decided to make a chapter of the content of our emails that flowed through the Internet.

CHAPTER 20

"Out of Calamity comes Contentment"

*

AS I SAID before, when I first began using a computer, I was mainly interested in working on my bible study lessons. Eventually, I learned how to send and receive email. I sincerely enjoyed communicating with my church family, family and friends. However, it never occurred to me for one minute that the Internet would lead me to a wife and a new life. Over a period of almost a year we began a friendship and then relationship that would last the rest of our lives. Here is a sample of those emails. I saved each one of them and soon was to learn that Carol was keeping a book of them as well.

During the terrorist attacks the whole country was in turmoil and this affected the airports—flights in an out . . . all airports were shut down immediately after September 11, 2001.

On Friday, September 14, 2001 2:48 PM, I received an email from Carol which read: "Hello Alphonso,—I just left a message on your answering service that I was sending an email as well. Lindsay said that on Wednesday you sent me a question, which I have not answered and please send it again. I went through the emails and can't find the question. As it turns out, I will be picking you up at the airport (still am unable to ascertain the flight status for Continental). Now I have a few questions for you—I will pick you up at the gate when your plane arrives. Would you like a wheelchair? What do you prefer to drink? Do you drink coffee? Debra does but I drink hot tea with cream & sugar. She makes good coffee I think, but have only heard that! As you serve the cause of Christ at Mount Morris, I want to serve you in His name in my house! <>< Carol"

If you know me at all you can only imagine what I felt at her question regarding the wheelchair. Carol still did not know my age and had heard that I had a lung removed and so she was concerned that I would not be able to walk the distance required in an airport!

I had to let her know by replying with this email a couple hours later! "Hello Carol—No, I will not need a wheel chair. Yes, I do drink coffee. I called Continental and they said yes, they would be flying Sunday, but for me to call them back Saturday and confirm the facts. Alphonso"

Later that evening she replied, "Hi Alphonso, I hope you weren't offended by me asking if you needed a wheelchair. Bobby said, "What! You asked him if he needed a wheelchair!" This is my late husband Bob's son and he said I might have asked the wrong thing. Oh my, I sure didn't mean to, just checking. Debra was happy to have another coffee drinker in the house for a week. What did you ask me that I haven't answered you yet? According to Lindsay, you said it was in an email from Wednesday. <>< Carol"

The following day I called the airlines and sent this email to Carol: "Hello Carol—My flight here in Texas is ok, but I cannot land in Dulles, so they have re-scheduled my flight to leave on Monday at 7:00 a.m. I will still arrive at Dulles at 2:38 p.m. on Monday. Alphonso"

I want to say here that at this point I had no idea regarding Carol, her personal status or her race. All I knew about her was that she was married to a black man and secretary of a black Baptist church in VA. Speaking of her being married to a black man, Deacon Robert Whitmore, I want to say more about the Whitmore family at this time.

While growing up in Hume, VA, I was well acquainted with the whole Whitmore family. I went to school with some of them, worked for and with some and my brother, Rev. James Burrell, was the best friend of Carol's husband, Robert Whitmore when they were coming up in school. My brother James and Bob were nine months apart in age. I was gone from the area when this relationship between Bob and my brother James was going strong. Prior to her marriage to Bob, he had asked her to visit his 'friend James' at the Annaburg Manor in Manassas VA. They went every week to visit him and had a picture taken on one of their last visits. Carol placed this picture on the refrigerator. She had become quite close to James during that time. She and Bob had brought a friend to Mount Morris Baptist Church for my brother James' Homegoing. I had the occasion to talk with Bob at the service but never saw Carol nor she me. I had no idea what she looked like and vice versa.

Sunday, September 16, I received this email from Carol regarding her duties as Secretary for the church: "Good Evening Alphonso, Please look at this below and send it back with any additions and corrections you want to make. Would you please try to do this tonight so that I can get up to the church and work on the programs for the revival services? You will have a long day tomorrow. We'll talk about that later. Here is part of what I plan to put in the program tomorrow . . .

"*Alphonso Washington is a legend in his own time. He preached his first sermon at Providence Baptist Church, Orlean VA over 60 years ago. He says, "If I live to see October 18, 2001—I will be 88 years old." In San Marcos, TX he remains a busy man. Still preaching when needed, he has been formally retired since July 1996. He leads a Bible Study in the Senior Center/Home where he resides. He no longer drives but that doesn't hold him back! He is well known in the community where he lives and is writing an autobiography! He comes from a long lineage of legends. Although Alphonso has been out of the Hume, VA area for over 50 years, he has well-known family here from the Cook's to the Poles, including Reverend James Burrell, his brother. Alphonso has out lived two wives who went on to Glory before him. They both died from cancer. He himself is a cancer survivor and continues to preach the Gospel and give God the Praise! He has three grown children and a grandson he raised from 4-days-old who proudly calls him Dad! The first-born was a girl named Mabeleen, who resides with her husband in Chico CA! He says, "Bet you can guess where she got her name!" Then son Samuel, who resides with his family in Falls Church VA—followed by Willie who resides in Nashville with his family. We rejoice that the Lord has led Rev. A. Washington back to Hume, VA for Revival Services preceding Homecoming."*

This was a very busy time for both of us. She was preparing the programs for the revival and Homecoming services and I was getting ready for a weeklong trip. Pastor Green was going to pick me up at the airport. Then between services Pastor Green told Carol that something had come up and he would not be able to do this. He asked if she would be able to do it instead. In the dining room she met Martha Green who asked if she knew what I looked like. Carol said she had no idea. Martha asked her if she knew Rev. Fred Poles and she said, "Yes!" Martha said, "Well he looks like Rev. Poles but that's all I will say, if Rev. Washington wants to add anything that is up to him!" That must have shocked Carol . . . nevertheless we talked later that evening and Carol asked me how she would recognize me (what was I going to wear) and what she should call me. I told her she could call me Alphonso or whatever else just so she didn't call me late for supper. I told her I would be wearing a white baseball cap and to meet me at the luggage pickup. She was near the bottom of the escalator when I heard my name called, "Alphonso!" I turned my gaze in the direction of the voice. You can imagine my surprise to see that she was white, and I was doing my best to hide it. My relationships in Virginia and Texas in my early years and mid life were filled with prejudices against me both as a 'Yankee' and a black man. Based on my experience during our first conversation by phone, however, I knew something big was going to happen and a change was coming.

We made our formal introductions and proceeded to get my luggage. She seemed surprised that I had packed four 26" Pullmans for this week in Virginia. She joked with me and asked if I was planning to stay a month. I assured her that a preacher needed to change suits often. Her children carried in my luggage for me to the guest room and as I passed by her refrigerator I saw the picture and remarked about it.

Shocking each one with these words I said, "What are you doing with a picture of my brother and Bob Whitmore on your refrigerator?" The first of many surprises that week.

On the opening night of revival, just hours after my arrival, my son Sam met us at a mall near Carol's home and followed us to the church. I was pleasantly surprised to see that my brothers and my sister on my Poles side were at the revival. Another shock came when I found out that Carol and Gladys Rector were close friends. Carol had called Gladys and wanted her to be at the revival because of the close association the Rector girls had with me in my early years in Hume and the surrounding area. This was the singing group that I carried with me when I traveled around to preach in that area. I had not seen Gladys in almost 59 years. Oh, it was a great night let me tell you. She and her sisters sang for me that night and it sure carried me back.

During the week I spent in Virginia, Carol took me anywhere I wanted to go to visit with my family members on the Poles side and to see cousins on the Washington side. She took me to all the old family homesteads in Hume and Ashville, and other places. My brother James and his wife Flora, who later had a dinner for me (more about that later) . . . I found out that my sister Viola and Carol were prayer partners at Mount Morris Baptist Church and loved each other very much. Carol knew nothing about me previously, and I did not know they were at all acquainted with each other! My sister Viola's husband Hugo was a best friend of mine long before they married.

Carol's daughter and other family members were more than kind to me during this trip. I met both of Carol's daughters, and they treated me with the love and respect that could only come from being raised in a non-prejudiced home. Their children were the same. We all became quite attached to each other in a family sort of way. Well, I love children, and her grandchildren were so loving and kind. Debra was to start a new Government job the day I returned to Texas.

This I must state, Mount Morris was not the same church that I left years ago. Not physically nor spiritually were they anything like I remembered.

My trip called for me to stay on past the Homecoming on Sunday after the revival. Homecoming at Mount Morris Baptist Church was a great day! There were at least four or five hundred people there. Many came to me that day and talked about times past and their remembrance of me and or my grandfather. I even had one woman, Violet, to come up to me whom I had not seen since I taught her in Sunday school when I lived in Loudoun County in the 40's. She was a small child then and happened to be a member of the church in which I was baptized, Mt. Olive Lincoln VA. She was currently a member of Trough Hill Baptist Church, which was pastored by Rev. Lindsay O Green twice a month.

After the successful revival and Homecoming, the night before my departure on Monday, I asked Carol and her daughter Debra to come into the living room for a talk. My mind had begun to switch from God's work to my personal feelings. I had not expressed anything about my own feelings and had pretty much buried them so that I could do God's work unhindered. During this conversation, I asked Carol, "Do you think you will ever marry again?" Her reply was, "No, I could live the rest of my life on the beautiful memories I have of Bob." I reminded her that she had told me God put her and Bob together, and if He did it once, could He not do it again? Her remark **was,** "Well, if you put it to me that way, I would have to say it's possible!" My point was that now that her formal year of mourning was coming to a close, men would begin to approach her, knowing more about her than she knew about them. She asked what I meant by that, and I told her that they knew three things about her; she was white and married a black man, she married an older man and she married a man like Bob, a man of great character and Godly qualities. She would know nothing about them . . . I warned her daughter to watch out for her mom and take care to protect her as she was a widow in the church. (As I told my son Sam later, I had to protect my interest in her, although no one ever knew my intention at this time.) We spoke regularly on the phone and exchanged emails:

After I returned to Texas, I sent this email to Carol—Monday, September 24, 2001 9:25 PM, "Hello Carol & family—I got home about six-o-clock; I spent over an hour at the airport with Kevin. I really did have a good good good time in Virginia. When you answer please send me Carolyn Green's Address and email I seem to have lost it. She called me about seven o'clock. Goodnight for now. Alphonso"

Later that evening I sent another email to her saying, "Hello Carol—I remember that all things work together for good; for them that love the Lord, and are called according to His purpose. What God has for His people is for them and they will get that which He has in Store. I sure did feel like family there and still feel like family. How is Debbie's cold? Is she better? I do hope they get a house soon as that is what all of you want. Carolyn Green called me about 7 o'clock; I seem to have lost her email address she gave me Friday, so please send it to me. As ever, Alphonso" You may notice that I sent these two emails very close together and signed them differently. This signature, 'as ever' represents the feeling that I had at the first phone call that Carol made to tell me of my arrangements to come to VA. I was now showing my feelings that went back to my first hearing her voice on the phone before I ever met her. She replied the next day, Monday, September 25, 2001 11:07 AM with this email, "Alphonso, Making Bean and Ham soup for dinner for the kids (Bobby and Debra) and this thought came to my mind. Remember when you asked Debra and me to sit on the couch in the living room for a talk . . . and you said, tell me this-do you think you would ever get married again? I answered you, no but you said, "Didn't you say God put you and Bob together and don't you think he can do it again?" I asked you the same question and you pretty much gave me the same reply, along with some very godly advice about what to look for in a husband. Is there someone in your complex or church to which you feel God is leading you in that direction? Being happy doesn't mean everything's perfect. It means you've decided to see beyond the imperfections. Praise God He looked beyond our faults and saw our need." Carol

It was at this time I decided to escalate my personal feelings towards Carol by phoning her during the week. We talked often during this first week mostly because my pastor was so sick and while he took up most of the energy in the conversations, he was not all. We learned more and more about each other, our children and personal habits. I knew that I would have to move quickly because at my age life comes at you fast and you don't waste time, you know what I mean? I was seeking a commitment from her, if at all possible! I knew she would be a praying wife, Lord willing.

On Friday, October 05, 2001 7:15 PM she wrote to me, "Dearest Alphonso,

> How good it was to hear your voice last night. You asked if you could court me! I remember saying 'from TX?' But I said YES! Please send me an email explaining the "4 Rights" you mentioned last night. How all 4 must be in place . . . I wanted to hear that again and right now I have forgotten what they were?
>
> Your friend always, forever, Carol"

It was really good to see this in her email to me; it was a promise of things to come. I wrote back to her in this email on Saturday, October 06, 2001 4:10 PM

> "Hello Carol—
>
> I am so very glad you called last night, because I have not got that email yet, and it is now 4:15 p.m. We sure got a lot of understanding and are on the same page, it seemed like for a while we were trying to see who could hold out the longest with making a true commitment. Now that we have both committed, it is time to talk about the many stumbling blocks that we must climb over; the best way to secure that obstacle is to allow God to take the lead. I really do not want to make any move that will cause any conflicts in our later years. I must prepare for Church tomorrow, as I have to preach. So I will close. Alphonso"

Not hearing from her later that evening I sent this email Sunday afternoon, the next day . . . "Hello Carol—I do thank you for your prayer for the service at First Baptist. I really believe that God heard and answered. Also I really needed prayer. This morning when I got to Church, the other preacher called the pastor's house and talked to the pastor's wife; she then got the pastor on the phone with him. The pastor said a few words then asked for me. I took the phone and he said to me, Reverend I am not doing well, and my white blood cells have not done well in two months. Tell the Church to Pray for me. This is the first time that he has admitted to me that he was not doing well. I called the Church in special prayer at the Altar. Then we had a great service, not many people but a great force of the Holy Spirit. I sent you an email that I started yesterday but I sent it today. With you having family, home and church ties in Virginia; and I with family in both Virginia, California, TX and TN then with Church ties here also I am very much at a standstill about what to do with our relationship at this point. I do want to do whatever God wants me to do; I think I told you on the way to the airport that I had a feeling that my trip up to Virginia was the beginning of something. Let us take our time and give God the lead; because with what we do we will surely need Him. But I will always remain God's and yours. Alphonso" Later that same evening I remembered a question that Carol asked and answered her:

"It's me again Carol,
I failed to answer your question about the four ways.

(1) The right thing
(2) The right way
(3) The right place
(4) The right time

If either one of these are in error the whole is wrong. Alphonso"

Speaking of this idea of the four ways, I must admit that Carol urged me to tell my children about our budding relationship but I didn't want to tell them of this for my own reasons. When I finally did, it seemed to cause them alarm. Carol told her children right along . . .

On Monday, October 08, 2001 7:02 AM I emailed Carol this note:
"Good Morning Carol—How are you this morning, well I hope; and ready to start a great day that the Lord has made, also to be glad in it. Here is a poem that I remember from my school years:

> "O sun and skies and flowers of June
> And flowers of June together
> Ye cannot rival for one hour
> October's bright blue weather
> When on the ground red apples lie
> In piles like jewelry shining
> And redder still on old stonewalls
> Are leaves of wood bound twining?
> When comrades seek sweet country hunts
> By twos and twos together
> And count like misers' hour by hour—
> October's bright blue weather.

There is one more verse that I cannot get together, but 77 years to remember school poems isn't easy. I learned this while in school with Annie Whitmore. Well, have a great day with much love. Alphonso"

Carol shared information about our relationship with two of her closest friends, Annie Whitmore Brown, who was also her sister-in law, and Carolyn Green, wife of the pastor of Mount Morris Baptist Church. Later, she decided to tell her friend Pauline Scott, with whom she had worked in Reston, Virginia, regarding what was happening between us.

To Pauline she wrote this email on Monday, October 08, 2001-

"Shhh! Pauline, my dear sister—this is so cute . . . he sent me this yesterday afternoon. He wanted to know if I would make a true commitment to him alone. I said 'yes.'

". . . With making a true commitment. Now that we have both committed, it is time to talk about the many stumbling blocks that we must climb upon; the best way to secure that obstacle is to allow God to take the lead. I really do not want to make any move that will cause any conflicts in our later years." Do you see the sentence that touched me so much? "I really do not want to make any move that will cause any *conflicts in our later years.*" Is that precious or what? Bob felt the same way. Neither of them saw nor see age as a hindrance in our relationship. That blows me away. God is so good He is faithful. It turns out when he was giving me advice about men who might approach me; he wanted me to consider him! Love ya! Carol

Hope you are enjoying your day.

Ps: You know I am keeping a diary of all this wonderful stuff "for our later years." Could God bless me with yet another Godly husband, twice in a row?"

I was able to get another email off to Carol Tuesday October 09, 2001 10:20 AM

"Subject: News"—"A blessed good morning to you! After a great night sleep and an early rising I'm setting out for a busy day. At 10:00 AM an appointment for maybe an hour and a half, then at 11:45 there is a City Wide Ministers Monthly Luncheon meeting that I should attend, but am not sure that I will be through with my appointment in time to make it. Then Sam and Barb are supposed to come from Corpus Christi Texas some time today; I do not know just what time to expect them. Enough about me, I do want to hear about you; and what life is doing with you, the family and that includes the Church. How are you spending the day there all by yourself, I hope you are not lonely and bored; and if so please tell me what I can do to change that. With love, Alphonso"

Carol wrote to Pauline again on the 12th of October, "I will be at Robin's wedding. Isn't it wonderful? Such a sweet couple . . . A and I have been talking last night. He wondered if Carolyn and Lindsay had any idea what has happened between us. Meaning he has asked me to make a commitment to him for a period of time. Right now he doesn't expect me to say anything because of the distance restraints. But he says God will make a way where there seems to be no way. He said he has the picture of he and I that Bobby took, up over his computer and Sam & Barbara came to visit yesterday to talk of some property he has that he wants to sell . . . it is a vacant lot. He said Sam looked up over the computer and he watched Sam's face as he settled in on the photo. But neither said anything. He felt that if Sam had stayed longer it would have come up. Then he said, "Getting back to Carolyn and Lindsay—how do you think Lindsay would feel if I took away his secretary?" I said I did not know . . . but I would be with my husband. He said I gave the right answer. But I will mention to him this morning that MM needs an Associate Pastor. One of the reasons he didn't attend MM was because they were/are? Primitive and he don't go for that way of thinking. I said I think Lindsay is trying to move MM away from that stigma, I believe. Am I right? Bobby and Debra know about what is going on. They are 100% supportive as long as I don't move to TX. This is a bunch of stuff to throw at you while you are so busy with the wedding. Are you at work or home? Looks like you are at work. Love you—please share your thoughts. The few I have shared are just a small part of our phone call last night. Carol"

Carol's friend Pauline responded right away with this email, "Yes. I am at work and WOW . . . I am so tickled! Goodness, I am speechless. To answer the question about MM: I don't think Lindsay is adhering to the OLD SCHOOL notions anymore. We ARE moving away from that (I hope). It is wonderful that the family is supportive. Umm . . . Assistant Pastorship? Now that's something to think about ☺ Nope . . . We can't lose you to Texas! He has to come up here. So there! I hope we get a chance to 'talk'. My mind is full of things that my 'fingers' can't articulate just now. I want to know all the things you talked about last night . . . love, P"

I sent this email to Carol later that night . . . "Hello Carol—I will now answer your question about what I meant, the thought came to me that if we're married and my life style remained as at present I would have to move you to Texas. Then your state of affairs came to mind; your Church affairs are greatly important to me. Tomorrow at 6:30 AM will leave to go to Caldwell Texas for our 10th District American Legion Meeting. I am not the District Chaplain anymore, but I am a delegate for the local Post. Yes I slept later this morning than usual. God is not through with us yet. So if we be patient He will work it out. Love You—More and More Alphonso"

Carol's friend Pauline responded with this email: "I think you are 'over-thinking' things. For one thing . . . You ARE obedient to God. Does that tell you anything? Just let things happen. They will either 'happen' or they 'won't. Take one day at a time. Get to know this man and as your relationship develops, let that tell you what you need to know. You already, pray. You already let the word of God lead you, You are 'already' IN this relationship; new that it may be. As for telling Pastor Green . . . Eventually, I think you SHOULD talk to him. But let him open the door and ask . . . He will, you know. He'll want to know if you've heard from Alphonso. You tell him yes, and at that time, share your developing relationship. ('My advice' only . . . you'll know what you need to do without it). You won't have to ask God to lead you. Keep walking and he WILL lead you. It's only when your feet aren't' moving that he can't direct your path . . . Luv P"

Saturday, October 13, 2001 5:50 PM I wrote this note to Carol, "Hello Carol

To answer your question, I do not have a middle name; I guess my parents thought Alphonso was enough. Since I will be out of town all day tomorrow I thought I would write you tonight; and wish you a great weekend. I am sure the grandchildren will be there tonight to spend the weekend. I just called my Pastor's house and another preacher's wife answered the phone, she said the pastor had just come in from the hospital, taking treatments, and was asleep. Tell Bobby and Debra and the children hello, and I still miss them. Have a good night rest, with much love. Alphonso"

Sunday evening October 14, Carol wrote, "I love this and am baking it right now!!!

"RECIPE FOR SUCCESS

INGREDIENTS:
1 PART OF KNOWING WHO YOU ARE
1 PART OF KNOWING WHO YOU AREN'T
1 PART OF KNOWING WHAT YOU WANT
1 PART OF KNOWING WHO YOU WISH TO BE
1 PART OF KNOWING WHAT YOU ALREADY HAVE BEFORE YOU
1 PART OF CHOOSING WISELY FROM WHAT YOU HAVE BEFORE YOU
1 PART OF LOVING & THANKING GOD FOR ALL YOU HAVE
(The "BAD" INCLUDED)

MIXING INSTRUCTIONS

Combine ingredients together gently and carefully. Using faith and vision mix together with strong belief for the outcome, until finely blended. Use thoughts, words and actions for best results. Bake until Blessed. Give thanks to God again.

Yield: Unlimited servings"

I couldn't resist keeping this particular email in the book, as it so describes Carol's spirit. I later replied to her following a phone conversation.

> "Good Morning Sweet Carol—I got your phone message Tuesday morning October the 16th, I was out walking when you called, and often I go walking between 8:30 and 10:00 o'clock, except Saturday and Sunday when the weather is good. I mailed you a package yesterday of some things that I thought might help you to help someone else. I hope I am getting all your emails, yet I have not got any since Sunday. I sent out an explanation of John 3:16, to all my addresses Monday. We really had a glorious time Sunday at Church, one of the pastors from Austin, a close friend of my pastor came down and preached; one of the persons that had been coming to Church each week since July cast his membership with us. The pastor is about the same. Some days he seems to get a little better and the next he seem to go the other way. How are you and the family? Say Hello to all the people there. I love you sincerely. Alphonso"

Between October and March the courtship part of our relationship began without the usual complications of physical contact; we were going to court in the old fashioned way. We got to know the heart and soul of each other through many hours of phone calls and emails and personal cards and letters. I asked Carol once if she could be attracted to me—her answer was yes! Her deceased husband was attracted to her by her spirit and joy and so was I. We were making plans for our meeting in March to meet family and measure the true compatibility of our love. But, I would not be staying with Carol this time. Plans were made for me to stay with her daughter Debra in Orlean VA.

One thing that I feel very strongly about is this: You don't mix your personal business with God's business. I had no way of expressing my feelings to Carol when I was there for revival. Even though I felt as I did the month before I came. We prayed every time we talked on the phone. It was great to hear someone pray with me for my family, she prayed for my grandson Kevin when 9/11 happened and I prayed for her son Joe and daughter Debra. They were all working in Washington DC when the plane hit the Pentagon.

CHAPTER 21

"The Courtship is in full Swing"

*

I CAME AS we had planned to Orlean VA in March of 2002, where I stayed with Carol's daughter and her husband, to formally meet all of Carol's family and court her properly. We spent about 10 days together during which time I asked the pastor and his wife to come to her house after church before I left to return to TX. We then told the pastor that we planned to marry in the summer. I asked Pastor Green, "Would you marry Carol and me?" He was surprised but said, "Yes, after 3 counseling sessions."

During this courtship period while we were together we went on eBay to look for rings. I had told Carol that I had $250 I could spend on a wedding set. EBay was the only way to go she said. It was a great time searching, she taught me how to search, but there is no chance I would do this without her help because of the accounts she had already set up. But we found a set on Saturday afternoon that we both really liked and she clicked a button to watch it. The ad read:

"This is a FABULOUS lady's 14K gold wedding set with a center diamond weighing approximately 30 points. On the wedding engagement ring there are sixteen channel set diamonds with the center diamond. On the matching wedding band are 27 channel set diamonds. Total weight is 130 points. All of the diamonds are clear white and sparkling. It is a size 5 1/2. Buyer pays $7.00 shipping and insurance. I accept PayPal and money orders."

The reason we didn't buy it then or bid on it was because it had a $375 starting bid. It was too much to make as an initial bid. After church on Sunday we came back to Deb's and Carol used her computer to check on it and the auction was over but the item was not sold. When she went home, she contacted the seller and asked if she could buy the set for $250. She explained our situation and the lady said yes. She called me at her daughter's later that evening to tell me what the lady said. I told her to buy it and that when I got home, I would send a check. She went ahead and used PayPal to buy it—it came from an estate in Florida.

Another treasure during this visit was the occasion of meeting Rev. Gillison Wanser, Pastor of First Springs Baptist Church in Warrenton VA.

His wife, Fannie and Carol had a great relationship that evolved from the same weekday prayer meeting in which Carol met my sister Viola. She had talked with Fannie and Fannie was excited to have me come out and spend time with them while I was there. This we did and oh, what a blessing it was for me to meet Rev. Wanser. We spent many hours together with him, 'picking my brain' and just getting to love each other in the Lord. I had casually met both of them when I came to preach revival but this time the meeting was so much sweeter. I came to find out that Rev. Wanser's birthday was the day before mine, Oct 17th!

* * *

We determined that May would be a good time for me to return for the counseling sessions. I came to stay in Hume, Virginia this time with my next oldest living brother, James Poles, following my first stop in Nashville for the graduation of one of my granddaughters in TN. It was a brief visit during the beginning of which Pastor Green said he would not be able to marry us after all. He told us this immediately upon our arrival at the church because he felt that since he wasn't going to marry us, we might not want to continue with the counseling sessions we had planned with him. This was a great shock to both of us because we had been looking forward to this time between March and May with Pastor Green. Pastor Green indicated that he had been told by some members of Mount Morris not to marry us while others said he should. Nevertheless, he said he was not going to marry us for personal reasons and to please not question him on them. We did not question him although Carol was quite upset that her pastor would not be marrying us. However I felt confident that God would have His way in this marriage. He asked if we desired to end the counseling session at that time. I told him that we would continue with the counseling. I decided it was best since he was Carol's pastor and would be mine as well. Following the first session of counseling, Pastor Green gave us some homework and we set a time to return the following day for the second session. He asked us to write down separately all the names of our children and beside each name to write how they felt about the upcoming marriage.

As we left with this seemingly terrible news that he would not marry us, I immediately took my bride-to-be (who was certainly upset by this turn of events) to see my younger brother Pastor Rev. Fred Poles, Mt. Zion Baptist Church in Boyce VA. Fred lives in Hume, not far from the church. I told Carol, "Baby, don't worry about what the pastor said, God will work this out."

When we got to Fred's house, I asked him if he would marry us on July 4th. Nothing could have prepared us for what happened next. Fred leaped up and down for joy and cried when asked if he would perform the ceremony, hugging us both for all he was worth. He said he would be "honored." It was really quite touching for Carol and me too!

The following day as we met for our second counseling session I told Pastor Green that my brother Rev. Fred Poles agreed to marry us. Carol still wanted to be married in her church so I asked the Pastor if this would be ok. He then told us that he would be out of state and but he knew Fred well and would turn the church over to him for the occasion. This was certainly a blessing to hear. I put my sister-in-law, Flora in charge of the dining room and reception. She had complete authority to work out all the details for us. We then discussed the names of our children and their thoughts with the pastor. Carol told him that her youngest son was concerned about the age difference and went to his pastor for advice. His pastor directed him to several passages of scripture which dealt with honoring your mother. He called her and told her we had his blessing. One of her daughters was concerned about the age difference as well, considering her previous husband, Bob died suddenly just 9 days before their 2nd Anniversary. This devastated Carol and her daughters knew what she went through and did not want to see her go through this again. They both came to love and accept her choice. My children did not know much until March when I began to let it slip out much to Carol's disapproval. She had wanted me to tell them about her all along but I refused. I believe all my children and their families love Carol to this day. All except my grandson who has never reconciled my marriage. We discussed this all with the pastor.

We returned the next day for the final counseling session at which Pastor Green seemed quite excited about how well they went. He said, "I have never counseled a couple so well prepared as you both are. You have certainly prepared for even the unexpected possibilities, having the horse in *front* of the carriage so to speak, while most have it the other way around." Pastor Green seemed to beam in his happiness for us. One thing we decided early on was that our marriage would not be a contract between us; our marriage would be a covenant before God. God honors His covenant keeping people.

Well, I closed out my business in San Marcos at Redwood Springs by the end of June 2002. The staff and residents got together and gave a lovely party for me (and Carol by proxy) that was centered on our up-coming marriage. A substantial sum of money was collected to help us get started in our "new life."

* * *

The sooner the better, I thought. We ended up having one week from which to pick a date. I had planned to be out of the Redwood Springs at the end of June. I would stay at James and Flora's house until the wedding. His wife, Flora had agreed to plan the food for the reception and organize it. A friend of Carol's worked for a large commercial ticketing company and had won a trip to a nice hotel, and she gave that to us for our honeymoon! In case you are wondering how we picked the date for the wedding, Carol had made arrangements a year earlier to have the Whitmore family reunion at her house the fourth Saturday in June. She wanted to be a Whitmore when she hosted this reunion. I wanted her to be a Washington for my family reunion in Front Royal the following weekend, the first Saturday in July. Her birthday is the 3rd of July and she didn't want to get married on her birthday so, we picked the 4th, a holiday for everyone, and we picked a morning wedding so that everyone could have a light lunch and move on with their own family get-togethers.

(In the first picture is Carol and her son, Joe, who gave her away to me. The second picture shows the wedding party, my son, Sam, Carol, me and her youngest daughter, Christy.)

We were married on July 4th 2002 at 10:30 AM between the Whitmore and Washington Family Reunions. Our honeymoon was cut short because on July 7th I wanted to join Mount Morris Baptist Church. We began our marriage on a run, and we have not stopped running yet.

Since we married, I have remained active. On July 21st my cousin Carolyn Green, the pastor's wife died at home on a Sunday morning while he was preaching. This was a tremendous shock to all of us. Pastor Green made a remark to me when he came home from the hospital. My wife and I were at the house to answer the phone and take messages for him. There were also a number of ministers and friends there. He said, "Who knows whether you are come for such a time as this!" We were standing in the living room holding hands and about to pray for him before leaving to go home. He was quoting from Esther 4:14. On the heels of the Homegoing of cousin Carolyn Green was my first introduction to the 2nd National

Ketoctan Baptist Association since I left Hume 60 years ago. Because of the negative experiences I had through my grandfather and Mount Morris Baptist Church, I did not have a high regard for 2nd National. The feelings I had for the past sixty years were greatly wrong on my part. The invitation to run a revival at Mount Morris was the beginning of a way to make a correction to my way of thinking and experience. Later that year, at a special called business meeting he told the church he would be taking a month long sabbatical in January 2003. He placed me in charge of church matters for the month along with the Deacon Board. During this time I preached my first funeral at the request of a church member. Her brother was going to be funeralized from a funeral home in Manassas, as he had no church affiliation.

In the next year, August 2003, I was asked to preach the opening Association sermon for the Thursday evening slot. I learned that the Association was in a bad location and some desired to move out but at a very slow pace. The Wanser's and Washington's soon began to run with each other. We went out to celebrate our birthdays each year and he gave me a standing invitation to preach one of the Sunday's of his vacation time. Carol and I spent many occasions at First Springs and I grew to love the Wanser's more and more. It is my desire that Rev. Wanser preach my Homegoing service here in Virginia; we are that close. A friendship grew out of my close relationship with my brothers Fred and James. They had a dinner and invited a pastor friend of theirs. At this dinner the preacher friend, Rev. Leonard Morton Sr. of First Baptist The Plains VA asked me to preach every 2nd Sunday in November for his Senior/Missionary Day program. Rev. Morton at has told me I am to show up at First Baptist every 2nd Sunday in November until . . . (I guess he means until I show up somewhere else!) Another great friendship began. The following year—2004, I preached for the Association again; this time my text came from Deuteronomy 2:3 which reads, "Ye have compassed this mountain long enough turn you northward." The whole Association present went wild over that sermon. It moved them into action. Only God could do that.

The same year that Carol and I married, she introduced me to the Full Gospel Business Men's' Fellowship International, Chapter 158 where I met and made many lasting friendships, like Bill Hines, the president, John Hoying and Rick White who were also officers. I served in the position as Chaplain in Warrenton, Virginia.

We began volunteering a period of time each week at the WorkPlace in Warrenton VA. I counseled the patrons after their intake and Carol would teach them how to prepare themselves for a job, and how to write resumes. We made lasting friendships with the staff and patrons and enjoyed this work two days a week. We continued this until the office closed its doors due to lack of funding.

At a regular business meeting of the church, my wife resigned as Superintendent and I was appointed to take her place. For two years I observed the operation of the Sunday school, while my wife was acting Superintendent and noticed the literature they were using was very deep and strong in its aim for the church; it did not seem to fit the needs of Mount Morris.

My first move, as Superintendent was to change the literature to RH Boyd Publishing Sunday school materials, a company I had been familiar with since my childhood days. Since the end of my first year with the Sunday school, the pastor has praised our Sunday school as being, "The best Sunday school in the county, no, the best in the state of VA, no the best in the whole country! It's second to none!" In addition to this ministry I am an Associate Minister of Mount Morris Baptist Church and now Superintendent Emeritus of the Sunday school, and Minister of Christian

(Picture of me giving the opening prayer during the opening of our Sunday School, taken in 2008).

Education. I joined the Second National Ketoctan Baptist Association of which Mount Morris is the mother church. Since joining the Association, I preached sermons for the evening service in August 2003, 2004, 2006 and 2009. I have served in several capacities at the Association and the Sunday school conferences. Through these past 6 years working in the Association the Vice Moderator called me "The Senior Statesman" of the Association. Since then he has become the Moderator, Rev. Arthur Greene of Swift Ford BC, which was my brother Rev. James Burrell's former church. One of his first official moves was to create a position called Senior Statesman and appoint me to that position. He received a standing ovation when he publically announced this to the Association.

I obtained my Virginia Clergy license August 9th 2005 and the same day I came home with the license, Carol's next door neighbor's son came over and said he would be 'honored' if I would marry him and his fiancé. God is still using this humble servant. I conducted another wedding for a couple in Bowling Green, Virginia, after becoming a "surrogate father" to a manager of Friendly's Restaurant where Carol and I dine frequently.

I continue to offer private counseling services and support the Poles family reunions as an active planning committee member, along with my niece Wrennetta Poles, her mother, Clara Poles (widow of my brother Charles), my wife and my son Sam. I still maintain contact with some of my dearest friends and associates in San Marcos and continue to counsel and aid them where needed. A couple of my long-time American Legion friends, the Tvrdiks have been coming to Warrenton every year since we married. Much to our delight we have also been visited by Dr. Elvin Holt, Texas State University at San Marcos, where he is Professor of English Studies, among other classes.

* * *

Pastor Green appointed me to chair a committee charged with building an addition to the church and bringing it into compliance with ADA standards. I am active in the Fauquier County & Vicinity Ministers Coalition. Carol has given up her post as church secretary at Mount Morris Baptist Church; she is *my personal* secretary. She worked for about 15 months to meet her social security requirements. We found out the hard way that working that job was a liability for us financially and this was one of the main reasons she let to it go.

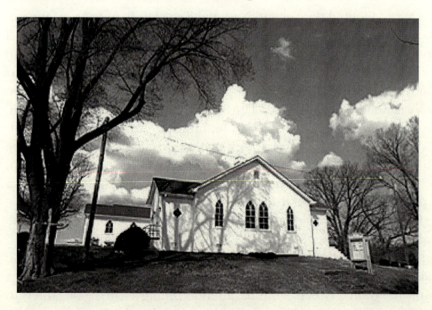

I plant a large vegetable garden each year. I supplied 18 heads of cabbage 2006, white potatoes, 2007 and sweet potatoes for our church Homecoming September 2008 (serving about 500). I credit John Whitmore with my tree planting success and gardening efforts. He taught me well. John was Carol's late husband's older brother. It is truly amazing how God joined the Whitmore family and Poles family to me in these, my grandest years. My grandfather taught me that when I plant my corn, I must always plant two for the black bird, two for the crow, two to pull up and two to grow; in addition to this, I plant another row or two for the church. It was a great success; the freezer is full now with these blessings. Our mums (bushes) out front one year were the largest anyone in the area ever saw. Carol bought me a John Deer Gator to drive over to the garden and around the property to tend to my many fruit trees and vegetables. What a blessing that has been! It has a hydraulic lift on the bed for dumping fertilizer or gravel (around the pool). Sometimes I pick up Carol and take her on a tour. She lets me drive on the two roads of our development but not on the highway because while I have headlights on my Gator, I don't have license plates. Ha! I have been able to plant 2 peach trees, 2 plum trees, and 2 apple trees. I have also planted one pear tree, which has not reached its fruit bearing time yet. We have an abundant squirrel community that enjoys our fruit as well. We just try to get it before they do. So far we have been unsuccessful with the apple trees! We find apples on the ground with little bites taken out of them and cast off. How wasteful these squirrels are! I have been working with Carol's roses, the climbing ones and constructed a trellis for them, out near the parking area off the driveway. They are truly beautiful in the spring!

 We have had two new cars since we married and made many trips, one back to San Marcos for Carol to meet the people she has talked with on the phone and learn more of my life there. We were delighted to stay with Ofelia Vasquez-Philo, one of my dearest friends. I want to say more about this trip later. Our second trip was to South Carolina to visit Carol's Aunt Pat and Uncle Jim. Our next trip in 2006/07 was to Florida to visit Carol's father and his new wife, not many people my age have a living father-in-law! We stayed at his place by ourselves; he was at his wife's place—right across the street from us!

 My trip to San Marcos holds many wonderful memories. Rev. Herman Foster, now deceased was a frequent telephone caller to my Warrenton home, and now along with others planned a reception for us at the Dunbar Center in San Marcos. He picked us up at the airport and took us for a great meal at Furrs. The reception was a lovely time, and many people from the past came forward and shared stories and experiences relating to me. It was almost like "This is Your Life, Rev. Alphonso Washington." I saw a number of people I had not seen in a while. One of my former bosses, Dick Montague shared an interesting story about how he warned my co-workers to watch out for me because I had had a heart attack. They all dragged me out of a building I was working in because I collapsed due to heat and smoke inhalation, and here I was standing up being honored and every one of those co-workers passed on before me. The mayor was there to present me with a Key to the City and named the day for me in San Marcos. Friends at the City Hall gave Carol a beautiful set of china in the Old Country Rose, Royal Albert English pattern. She loved the gifts and treasures the thoughts and love behind them.

Tom Tvrdik, Commander of American Legion Post 144 presented me with a picture of the original 32 charter members of the black unit of the Post 144A. All have passed on but me. (Through the years, Tom and his wife, Sandy have become dear friends.) Harvey Miller had many pictures to share from past newspaper articles and Rev. Kyev Tatum spoke of our work with the Mitchell Community Center, and Rev. Foster spoke of our long friendship as well. Tom and his wife Sandy took Carol and me to all the churches I pastored, to Austin and to the American Legion convention in Bastrop, Texas. We also had a lovely dinner and visit with Nancy and Charles Ellis, among many others. I was so proud for Carol to meet my people in San Marcos, and they were so good to her.

With the many events that have happened since my return to Virginia, my marriage, the subsequent growth of my family, to include Carol's four children and their spouses, her eleven grandchildren, and one great grandchild, I could write another whole book. But right here, before I go on any further, I want to mention a significant help to me made by my brother Fred and his wife Gladys.

One Saturday in the late spring of 2005, I was gardening in the flower beds out front, when I suffered severe chest pains. Carol was in town at the time and when she came home, I did not tell her about this. After taking my nitro tablet, I felt better. The following day, after we returned home from church, I mentioned this to her, in passing. She was quite upset with me, for letting this go so long without letting her know. The next morning, she called the VA Clinic in Stephens City for an appointment. We got one right away and off we went. When I got there they immediately gave me an EKG, called an ambulance, which came take me to Winchester Memorial Hospital as they had no room for me at the Martinsburg WVA VA Hospital. Both Carol's daughters came that first night to visit me. It was not long before my son, Sam and grandson, Kevin came as well. The following morning, we had to make the decision to have me transferred to the DC VA Hospital or keep me there, under my Medicare insurance plan. Failing the stress test, they decided it was necessary to do a heart catheterization. Now the people from the finance office came to see us regarding the money that was necessary to remain in Winchester and have this procedure done. Right before these two women came into my room, my brother Fred and sister-in-law, Gladys came to visit me. She had just come from having a pacemaker put in. Because they were sitting on the couch in my room, the ladies asked that they leave, due to the personal nature of the finances they wanted to discuss. I told them Fred was my brother, that they were to remain if they so chose, which they did. While the ladies presented the financial case set before us, we were looking at a minimum of $900 to $1000 dollars that we would need to pay, before I left the hospital. This was difficult for us because we just didn't have that kind of money laying around. Fred leaned over and said something to Gladys, then told the ladies that it would be taken care of immediately. He said, "Go ahead and do all that is necessary to care for my brother, we will take care of the initial expense." At this point, Gladys wrote out a blank check to me, signed it and gave it to Carol, telling her to call Fred later with the amount she needed to fill in. I really can't express what a tremendous relief this was, that Carol would not be burdened with coming up with this unplanned expense. God placed Fred and Gladys in my room at the same time that the financial people came in and He moved in their hearts to take care of this matter for me. I am grateful for that generous display of love and care for me, given by my brother Fred and his wife.

  The rest of that story, as they say, is the following morning Carol's daughter, Christy, came to stay with her, while I had the heart catheterization procedure. Now I was no spring chicken, being 91, and one of the oldest patient upon which this heart doctor had operated. After it was finished he came out with 6 pictures of my heart and sat down with them to discuss the results. He was amazed at how 'clean' my heart was from any calcification deposits and showed the proof that in my lifetime I sustained one heart attack and no more. He told them that he had patients far younger than me, whose hearts were far worse than mine. He proceeded to tell Carol and Christy that I had a blockage in one artery but that my body had created its own bypass with four lateral veins. The other blockage was so slight that it was not even necessary to put in a stent. He told her to tell me, "Whatever your husband is doing, he should keep on doing it."

* * *

To help you further understand the nature of events since coming back to Virginia, I want to mention another serious event that happened on our most recent trip to Florida to see Carol's Dad and his wife. We returned from a 2.5 month trip to Florida in mid March 2008. This was the longest trip we have ever taken thus far. While it was exciting from the viewpoint of seeing family Carol missed, there turned out to be a whole lot of excitement because it was plain to see that God had placed us there to be a help to others.

In August of 2006, Carol's father remarried to a very sweet woman I call Momma Louise. During the winter of 2006/7 we stayed one month at my father in law's house across the street and spent every day with them. Upon our getting ready to return home from this trip, Carol's dad asked me if we would stay at least 2 months next year. I surprised even myself and said yes. We often say yes or no to one thing for a certain reason and then it turns out to be for quite another! God placed us in Florida for a specific purpose regarding dad and Momma Louise.

On the day we arrived, even the very hour . . . we learned that her dad was in the VA Hospital with chest pains . . . he is in 4th stage congestive heart failure and has angina. We did not understand what put him there. Momma Louise returned to pick up some personal items to take back to him and we happened to be there, having just arrived . . .

She burst into tears and told us where dad was and we wanted to go immediately to see him but she assured us that he was ok and resting. She would take us later that evening after she returned from carrying his toiletries to him.

In the meantime I unpacked the car and we were sitting in the living room waiting for her to return. I saw a car drive up in their driveway across the street from dad's house. I went across the street thinking it was Momma Louise and it turned out to be her son, Joe whom we had never met.

Joe immediately opened with, "Is she driving you crazy yet?"

Carol responded, "No, she is adorable and sweet!"

He began to curse her and say things that made my hair curl—about his own mother . . . I asked him to come across the street to talk with us in private. He continued to verbally abuse her, called her every kind of name, talked about how unfit she was, and that neither she nor Carol's dad should be driving and where was she, anyway? I was shocked and of course Carol was too! I told him where she was and that she would be back shortly. He immediately took out his cell phone called her in the hospital and cursed her out, half the time calling her mom and the other calling her Louise. It was truly shocking. When he hung up I asked him for his phone number and he went to get a business card from the car. Carol and I discussed this and decided we had heard all we wanted to hear out of this man and we would not to let him back in the house. When Joe returned with his card, we met him in the doorway and Carol said, "My husband is quite upset . . . he being a minister and both of us used to being around church people and other friends of good character, we were not used to such language and talk about one's mother." He blanched in front of us and appeared to be stunned at this news and said he had no idea . . . He then proceeded to tell me that he had connections in the police department and sheriff's department and he was going to have her license taken away . . . it took us three days to get to tell them what had happened. Dad came home and Carol and I went over to tell them or rather warn them that we met Joe and he said he was going to see to it that Momma Louise's license was taken . . . then the story of the past 20 years began to spill out like water over a dam broke loose, you catch what I mean!

Since her husband died in 1988, Momma Louise's son Joe took over her life or tried to. He took out credit cards in her name, put his name on her bank accounts, 'borrowed huge sums of money and never paid it back. He was the one in control of the credit cards and when he ran her so much in debt, he filed bankruptcy in her name to eliminate his bills/debt. A friend of hers died and paid for a new car for her . . . a 2000 Buick Century. Joe needed to borrow the car in 2003 (it had 15K miles on it then) and titled it in his name (using a power of attorney) and never returned it. He had her sign papers that were "in her best interest," he said that ended up giving **him** control of her health decisions. Prior to Carol's dad's marriage to Momma Louise she signed a pre-nuptial agreement separating their financial lives for the sake of the families. Joe saw this document and took it to a lawyer friend of his. Within 6 months after their marriage, he borrowed $7K from Carol's dad, giving him pre-signed checks made out to him in the full amount (one a month until the debt was paid) and later come over in the evening and took them to see his lawyer friend who had made corrections to Louise's will. (She had asked him to make a name change on her will since she had married.) It turned out he/and the lawyer slipped papers in the middle and she ended up signing a quitclaim deed over to her sons. She has another son in NC who also signed off on the deed. Since then Joe has been slowly been attempting to get her committed or out of the house, which would put dad back in his house.

This was the guy we met our first day here in Dec. 07, her own son, and we were stunned. Carol's dad and Momma Louise attempted to look into a reverse mortgage for her since Carol's dad's health is failing he was becoming really concerned about what would happen to her if he were not there. They had kept all this abuse to themselves. The lawyer who received the request for the reverse mortgage called them back and told them she did not own the home, her sons did. You can't imagine how devastated she was. They were both shocked. Neither one remembered signing anything but a will that was to only have her name changed. Carol's dad ended up in Bay Pines VA Center with angina again, chest pains more severe. A week after that shock, she got the notice that she was to surrender her driver's license to the DMV and retake the test to get it back.

Carol's dad ended up in Bay Pines again, a third time. This time he asked to see the psychologist. She recommended that he call the elder abuse hot line. After we got home he asked Carol to make the call and make the charge. Saturday an investigator came out and made an assessment. Momma Louise is in early stage Alzheimer's. We saw an attorney who sent us to another. The following week we went to see him again to sign papers. Jim, Carol's brother has been coming down to go with them as well as us. Jim has Dad's power of attorney and is executor of his estate so he really needed to be there and we were leaving on March 5th to go home to VA. Not being Florida residents there is little we could do in a legal sense. This lawyer seems to feel there is definitely been abuse of her finances, emotional well being etc and will take this case. We all went back to sign papers and talk details.

February 22, 2008 was Momma Louise's birthday (81) and this is the day her son arranged for her turn in her driver's license and take a test... it was awful what went on there. Finally we were getting somewhere but I was concerned about the reaction of Momma Louise's son, Joe. He is very volatile. He was responsible for putting Carol's dad in the hospital with angina 2 times from stress while we were there, with the things he is doing to his mother and upsetting her dad. He had taken her car, all her money, now her house. He cannot talk to her or about her without cursing her and she is the dearest little woman. She's feisty though. Oh, did I mention that Joe is a traveling salesman and very persuasive and demanding in his personality. As I said, his goal is to get her committed and take over her house. She says he is very greedy. Once he saw dads pre-nuptial he decided to get his name on her house so they could not use it to enter an assisted living center. He wants Dad to be responsible and since she signed these papers separating their estates, he is staking claim on her things ahead of time. On her birthday, Carol and Sam, Momma Louise' brother, took her to the DMV. Carol went in with her and they had an hour-long consultation with an examiner, a woman who taped the entire session. The bottom line there was that after they told the whole story to the examiner, she saw no reason to take her license at that time! Praise God.

The lawyer wrote to both sons, demanding the return of the house to their mother. I am writing this because I am happy to report that there is a wonderful ending to this awfulness! Dad told me that upon receipt of the letter, both sons put the house back in her name. Their lawyer was sending the new title/deed to the house in her name. The checks that were given to dad to pay back the $7K have not been paid back yet!

You just don't know what is going on in the lives of your loved ones! God placed us there in Florida for a reason. He placed us there for a long enough time because what we would have to deal with would take us some time. To be a witness to abuse and to build up the confidence of Carol's dad and Momma Louise to talk about what was happening, what had happened and allowed us to get involved to help restore this woman's shattered life. Glory to GOD! He is worthy of all the praise.

I encourage you to KNOW what is happening with your loved ones from whom you are separated and make sure that no one or nothing is breaking them down mentally or physically or financially! When I think about this ... well, most importantly God saw that we would be down here in the thick of what's going on to be a help to both of them.

* * *

Now this sort of thing has been happening, right along since we have been married. Starting with the death of my cousin three weeks after we married until now, some seven years later in July 2009, you can understand why I say, what we have seen and done would fill another book!

While going over my life's journey, some current events jogged my memory back to the days when I was working for the Amblers. Today we are experiencing a struggling economy because of a failure of Wall Street and its effect on Main Street. Another similar factor is that we have elected a new president, Barrack Obama, the first African American to be elected to this office. This is a similar economical situation that was occurring right before Roosevelt was elected. This situation carried on throughout his tenure as president. Roosevelt then was to take office inheriting a massive problem such as Obama has today. Now what I am about to say is what you might call hearsay. You see I worked for the Amblers during the Great Depression. I served this family and their guests at the dinner table and believe me, there was table talk. There was lots of talk about the events going on regarding the stock exchange, which I really knew nothing about. But I did know that Ned Amber was president of a bank in Warrenton and once Roosevelt became president in 1933, his first act was to deal with the nation's banking crisis. So what is going on right now in January 2009, reminded me of these times with the Amblers during the Depression. I remember hearing the table talk while daily serving breakfast, dinner and supper. They talked all the time about this first act of Roosevelt after his inauguration to close all the banks for one day and then set a plan in effect to keep each individual's withdrawals limited to a certain amount. The Amblers were very wealthy people who were greatly affected by the Depression. While I was still working for them they sold two paintings to a friend of the Hinkle's, the pastor of Leeds Manor Episcopal Church who came to dinner frequently. The Hinkle's daughter Jane and Elizabeth were good friends so the two families spent time together. The Hinkle's told their friends that the Amblers had these paintings. They came to the Amblers and purchased them both for $50,000.

As I finish this part of my life, I think about one of my favorite songs sung by my brother, Rev. James Burrell—

The song "I Can't Complain" says:
I've had some good days. I've had some hills to climb.
I've had some weary days, and some weary nights . . .

But when I stop and start to think things over.
All of my good days, they outweigh my bad days
so I can't complain.

That says it for me . . . because I often think of the blessings both Carol and I would have missed, had we not moved our lives forward, once again. I can't complain.

Get Published, Inc!
Thorofare, NJ 08086
19 October 2009
BA2009232